LORI'S LESSONS

to Dottie   12/13
  Your help has been most
successful to my well-being
to this point. Don't stop
believing!
                    Love
                    Lori

LORI'S LESSONS

WHAT PARKINSON'S TEACHES ABOUT LIFE AND LOVE

Carol Ferring Shepley

iUniverse LLC
Bloomington

Lori's Lessons
What Parkinson's Teaches about Life and Love

iUniverse books may be ordered through booksellers or by contacting:

iUniverse LLC
1663 Liberty Drive
Bloomington, IN 47403
www.iuniverse.com
1-800-Authors (1-800-288-4677)

ISBN: 978-1-4917-0217-8 (sc)
ISBN: 978-1-4917-0218-5 (hc)
ISBN: 978-1-4917-0219-2 (e)

Library of Congress Control Number: 2013916004

Printed in the United States of America

iUniverse rev. date: 10/24/2013

To Bob,
For all the things you've done for me. You are my life.
Lori

To Lori and Bob Patin, who have taught me about living life to the fullest, and to Jake, Callie, Lucy, and Mimi with love and gratitude, as always.

CONTENTS

INTRODUCTION

LORI PATIN IS A BEAUTIFUL woman with high cheekbones, luminous skin, and blonde hair. I expected to see her hand tremble, but it held steady as she walked slowly but gracefully to the car. When we got there, she told me with a little laugh, "I hope you don't mind sitting in the backseat because I have motion sickness, and I will vomit if I don't sit in the front." I hastily told her the backseat looked good to me.

I first met Lori and Bob Patin on June 14, 2012, at a train station on Parkinson Street in Normal, Illinois. The hand of destiny seemed to have a grip on these names because Lori has had Parkinson's disease for fifteen years, since she was fifty-five, and she works very hard to lead a normal life. Parkinson's is a progressive, still incurable, degenerative disorder that affects the central nervous system. But she challenges the progression in the most inspirational way and bets on a cure, determined to buy time until one is found.

Although I did not know it when we set up our meeting, a benevolent fate had brought us together. The Patins and I were meeting to see if we could work together. They wanted to assess whether I could write their story, and I wanted to find out whether their story intrigued me enough to commit a year of my life to it. In the few weeks between the time setting up and the actual meeting, my youngest daughter was diagnosed with epilepsy, a neurological disorder that has affected everything about her life and therefore mine. Time and again as our family has confronted the challenges of my daughter's condition, I have thought about what Lori would do in my daughter's case and what Bob would do for my own sake as caregiver. I have been inspired by their good example and feel so blessed that Lori and Bob have entrusted me with telling the story of all that they have learned from her determined encounter against this terrible neurological disease. It has strengthened me in our own encounter with disease.

In fact, it is a miracle that Lori was even able to meet me in Normal. Three years ago, she couldn't have made the trip because of her shaking palsy. The summer before last, her weight was down to 94 pounds from a normal weight of 110. After falling repeatedly and suffering hallucinations, she was hospitalized and lapsed into a coma. The standard medical wisdom has it that people with Parkinson's only get worse, but Lori has refused to accept that. Through a combination of tenacity, spirituality, hope, and what seems to some to be magic, she has done something remarkable: She has reversed the disease. On the Hoehn and Yahr Scale, a scale commonly used for measuring the degenerative effects of Parkinson's, last summer Lori was a 4.5 out of 5, 5 being the worst. Today she is a 2.5. Her mantra has been, "I am absolutely determined that this is not going to get to me. I will not let Parkinson's control my life. My destiny is still in my own hands." Her doctor, Michael Rezak, a specialist in the field for thirty-five years and a nationally recognized expert, knows of no one else with Parkinson's who has come back the way Lori has.

Her story is about much more than her struggle against this ugly disease; it is also the story of someone who has faced a terrible challenge, met it head-on, and refused to concede. And in the struggle, she has learned valuable lessons about life itself.

It is also a love story. Her husband, Bob, stands besides her in the fight, saying, "We both have Parkinson's." He takes tai chi and ballroom dancing with her. Every morning he brings her breakfast in bed and then washes and blow-dries her hair. Most of all he believes in her and her tenacity and determination. He says, "This disease is a teacher, and both Lori and I have surely struggled with some of the lessons, but we have learned the hard ones. The harder they are, the more we learned to team up against the challenge." He feels that PD (Parkinson's disease) is also their whole family's disease and that the battle has deepened their collective bond. Lori says, "I would not be alive without Bob." Bob says, "I wouldn't want to live without her."

Ever since Dr. James Parkinson first described the "Shaking Palsy" in 1817, PD has continued to be diagnosed the same way, clinically. That is, the doctor makes the diagnosis based on observation of signs and symptoms because there is no definitive lab test for Parkinson's, only tests to eliminate other probable causes. On her initial visit to his office, Lori's specialist, Dr. Rezak, believed she most likely had PD. "With twenty years of experience, I recognize the symptoms." A physician suspects Parkinson's when he or she sees two of the four primary symptoms: tremor, rigidity, slowness, and loss of balance. These symptoms can be subtle, and a healthy person can certainly experience some or all of them from time to time.

While all PD patients experience the disease differently, degeneration generally progresses slowly. One of the first symptoms, even before the characteristic tremors start, is loss of the sense of smell. Parkinson's symptoms always attack one side of the body first; they seized Lori's left side. Over time, people with PD will lose automatic movements such as blinking, smiling, and swinging the arms while walking. Their faces can become so lacking in expression that this symptom is known as the Parkinson's mask. As it grows harder to control fine hand movements, handwriting becomes smaller and more difficult to read. Speech becomes slower, quieter, and more of a monotone. PD can cause REM (rapid eye movement) sleep disorder that causes unique sleep disturbances where dreams seem real and are acted out. For example, Bob once woke to Lori choking him with his sleep apnea cord. It was nothing personal; she was just acting out a dream about walking the dog.

As the disease progresses, the advanced sufferer often shuffles and walks as if bent over at the waist with feet pigeon-toed. In advanced stages, the patient can experience hallucinations, difficulty swallowing, "freezing" (an inability to move), and even dementia.

Because there is as yet no known cure for Parkinson's, the goal of treatment is to minimize symptoms. But this was not possible before 1968. That was the year when Levodopa, or L-Dopa, was introduced, bringing relief for movement disorders, when no medication yet existed to treat Parkinson's symptoms.

L-Dopa sends dopamine back into the brain. On a biochemical level, a dearth of dopamine in the brain causes the disease. Dopamine is a neurotransmitter that sends signals to other parts of the body to control movement, among other things. The death of dopamine-generating cells in a region of the midbrain known as the substantia negra is what causes the motor symptoms of Parkinson's. It is believed the disease starts in nerve cells in the gastrointestinal tract and then travels up the spinal cord to the brain. By the time symptoms manifest, dopamine-generating cells have been 80 percent destroyed.

Today a constellation of medications combats the effects of Parkinson's disease. Even though no cure yet exists, there is lots of great, ongoing research that holds out hope for one. In the meantime, buying time is what matters.

In addition to taking her particular combination of meds, Lori combats her symptoms by dedicating as much as four hours a day to a rigorous exercise program that starts before breakfast. She also seeks help and treatment from a plethora of caregivers. Deep spirituality undergirds her, and the love of her husband, daughters, family, and friends supports her. Reaching out to help others with PD enriches her life. Most important, she has something nonquantifiable, which could be called a positive attitude, that keeps her hopeful. Bob says, "One of the things I find so compelling about her influence is how quietly she's pulled others into the circle of those dedicated to helping her beat this thing."

Last summer, on her way home from rehab after she came out of her coma, she said, "This happened to me for a reason. I have a feeling God wants me to do something with this."

Lori, under great pressure from her family, friends, and caregivers, decided to seek me out to write this book so she can share the lessons that her struggle has taught her and her family, lessons so much broader than fighting a disease, lessons about the mystery and challenges of life itself. She hopes they will help others dealing with their own great challenges. Lori says, "If they hear my story, they may take heart. I want them to think, *If she can do it, so can I.*"

Thus, her story.

Carol Ferring Shepley

CHAPTER 1

Lori's Life

LORI PATIN SAYS, "I AM a very lucky person—within a very unlucky situation. You might find it strange that I say this considering that I have had Parkinson's disease for more than fifteen years. Perhaps you will come to agree when you get to know me better. While I would surely love to be free of this disease, there have been blessings along the way. And hope ahead. If you or someone you love faces something awful, something that tries to tear your world apart, I offer my story in the hope that you will find encouragement here."

She was born Lori Cedik in 1942 outside Cleveland, Ohio. All four of her grandparents emigrated from Czechoslovakia. Her husband, Bob, likes to say she is a pure-blooded Bohemian— unique and exotic in his imagination. Not surprisingly, her family was very "old school," in the European sense. Her parents were strict, and as part of their family culture, they spent a lot of time together with grandparents. Both her mother's and father's parents lived on farms. Her younger brother, Don, and she, along with their parents, spent almost every weekend visiting one set of grandparents or the other. Sometimes they would just go for a meal, but often they would stay over Saturday night.

While Lori's mother's parents did not earn their living by farming, her father's parents had a very successful farm, with large orchards, where they grew apples, peaches, plums, and cherries. Their family often helped Grandfather with harvests because he needed extra hands.

He also had a vineyard and even made his own wine. For special occasions, he went down to the dirt-floor cellar and took a dusty bottle from under the stairs. When he took the top off the bottle, smoke drifted up. Then everyone had to drink a little glass, even four-and-eight-year-old Don and Lori. It was horrible.

Her grandfather prided himself on using the most up-to-date agricultural methods, including spraying his apple trees to protect against disease and blight.

Unfortunately, those "happy days" have come back to haunt Lori. Parkinson's disease occurs more frequently in farm families. Experts find an increased incidence among people with exposure to agricultural chemicals.

Lori Cedik was a good student and the kind of child who liked to please her parents and teachers. She was diligent and determined early on that she wanted to go to college. Today, a family would be proud of a daughter with ambitions like that, but Lori's parents, especially her father, were shocked. No one in her family had a higher education except the father, who had gone to a kind of engineering trade school. When she told him she wanted to become a lawyer, he said, "No. Girls are not lawyers. Girls are mothers."

So, painfully and reluctantly, Lori put that dream aside but would not give up on going to college.

She told him, "I am going to college."

"Well, how are you going to pay for it?" he asked.

"I will find a way."

When Lori earned a scholarship to Muskingum University, he said she would have to pay for the rest of her tuition and living expenses herself. Yet when the time came, he paid for them anyway. He was "old school" and stubborn, but in the end, his love for Lori trumped a long-held bias toward women. Father and daughter both ended up growing through the experience. Lori was proud of him for changing his chauvinist ways, and in turn, he taught her a lesson about the importance of changing long-held beliefs when it matters for someone you love.

When Lori graduated from Muskingum University, he was also one proud parent. "He didn't put it to me in so many words, but I knew. I often overheard him talking to his friends about his daughter who graduated from college, the first person in our family to do so," she said.

At Muskingum, Lori met Bob Patin, her "current and only husband." She says, "I have to admit that at first I did not care for him at all."

Freshman year they went with a group to ski in Pennsylvania. Even though everyone was all jammed into one small car, Lori didn't speak to him. "I made up my mind he was full of himself—without even saying a word to him." She kept running into him at different things over the course of the next two years, but she always thought, *Oh my gosh, somebody ought to tell him that he isn't as great as he thinks he is.*

To be completely candid, however, Bob thought Lori was "a gorgeous but snotty broad who dated all the wrong guys in the wrong [i.e., rival] fraternity." As it turned out, they both were in for a surprise.

Senior year, needing a date for a concert, Bob asked one of his best friends, Terry, for ideas because Bob's then-girlfriend had just given him back his fraternity pin. Terry suggested Lori because he knew she had also just been through a breakup so she would be available. When he called, Lori didn't want to seem overanxious. In fact, she probably wouldn't have gone at all if she hadn't just broken up with her boyfriend. Also, Bob invited her to a Four Freshmen—her favorite group—concert.

Lori says, "Then I did a terrible thing. I debated whether I should accept him or not with my sorority sisters. While he was still on the phone! Holding the receiver out so he could hear!"

"Pretty demeaning," Bob says. The consensus among the sisters—which Bob heard—was, "What do you have to lose?"

Bob had to get back at her somehow. So when he showed up at the Delta Gamma Theta house, he brought dead flowers. It looked like a bush.

She thought this was hilarious. "It was the best date of my entire life."

What a shame. It was April, almost the end of their senior year, and they had wasted all that time disliking each other. From then on, they spent every possible minute together. It was frenetic, attending fraternity parties, going to movies, even doing silly things like cow tipping (big in Ohio!). In fact, they enjoyed themselves so much that Bob almost flunked trigonometry.

Lori says, "Good thing he managed to pass, because without it, he wouldn't have graduated. We even broke the Delta Gamma Theta rules big time by meeting on the sorority house fire escape after hours. He didn't have a lot of sense: he wore a bright white shirt and white shorts on a night with a full moon. It was as if he wanted to attract the campus police's attention."

"Courage trumps intelligence," Bob says. "And hormones do too. We had a lot of chemistry going for us."

They even went "turfing," where you sneak out to the fifty-yard line on the football field and get personal. "My father had been so strict with me that I was grounded if I was as much as five minutes late coming home from a date. I thought, *Dad, you ought to look at me now.*"

Lori says, "I guess I tripped over the line into respect for Bob when, at an off-campus party, he poured his drink out into a bush, saying he'd had enough. I said to myself, 'Wow. That is really responsible. Maybe I've got a keeper.'"

Luckily, Bob's first job with Connecticut General Insurance (now known as CIGNA) was in Cleveland. Since Lori was home for that summer of 1964 after graduation, they got to see each other all the time for several months. He shared a one-bedroom apartment with nine other guys. They cleaned it twice a year, whether it needed it or not. You couldn't even see the floor of the kitchen. One time she said she would make dinner for him. It took her about two hours to get the kitchen clean before she could cook because it was stacked with pots and pans—"dirty, all of them dirty."

Time was fleeting and precious, but come August, they both knew she was going to leave home and drive out to California on Route 66 with her sorority sister and roommate-to-be. She'd signed a contract to teach school in Oxnard, a town north of Los Angeles. Bob had done his best to talk her out of going, but it was about duty and commitment. She'd made a promise. A lot of people break contracts, but not Lori. And that too is part of her story with Parkinson's because she has a contract with that disease as well. But she will share that later.

During those nine months teaching junior high, Lori only saw Bob twice. They spent almost all their money on long-distance phone calls. Bob called them "horny phone calls."

When he came out to California for Thanksgiving, he proposed and she accepted. Nevertheless, neither wanted to be lonely, so they had an agreement that they could both keep dating other people, Lori in California and Bob in Ohio, to test their commitment. "That gave me a few anxious moments, and I know it did the same for him," Lori says.

In Lori's close family, the grandparents continued to play an important role. After Bob visited her dad to request Lori's hand in marriage, he went out to her grandfather's farm to ask him as well, as was the tradition in the family.

After Bob requested his permission, her grandfather said, "I welcome you to the family, but no little ones for the time being." Then Grandfather broke out some of his famous homemade wine, Bob pretended to like it, and the die was cast. So Lori came home from California.

They were both still very sure about each other and got married on August 14, 1965, in Rocky River, Ohio. Lori was raised "sort-of Lutheran," but Bob's family was very serious about their Catholicism, so much so that the young couple had to be married in the Catholic church to make them happy. Even though Lori's grandparents had basically been run out of Czechoslovakia by the Catholics, they understood that this was her choice. The local Catholic church Bob's family attended was very strict and wouldn't allow them to play the "Wedding March" for the ceremony, but the service was lovely nonetheless.

The only problem was that the ceremony took place in the late morning, and the reception wasn't until evening. It was the hottest day of the year, and she wore her wedding gown the whole time. With all those hours to kill, friends started drinking. By the time the reception started, they were flying. Bob and Lori did their best to catch up. Some of her sorority sisters took over these enormous decorative cages in the reception hall so they could become go-go dancers.

Lori says, "I am sure my parents were thinking, *We paid for this?*"

After they married, Lori taught a year in Cleveland before they moved to Hartford, Connecticut, where Bob was transferred. There they spent the next fourteen happy years. Once settled, she pursued her love of literature in graduate school at Trinity College. She enjoyed her classes, but in one sense, Trinity was quite strange. Since it was still an all-men's college at the time, women graduate students were only allowed on campus at night. Lori quit just shy of her master's degree because they didn't have a lot of money at the time. She went to work for Connecticut General for a few years, working in the group contract department writing insurance contracts. She was proud that the English major was earning the money for their first house.

All the while, she was trying unsuccessfully to get pregnant. After she had a small surgical procedure, "everything worked fine. Bob says it was because we got a new mailman."

Alyson, called Aly, was born in 1971, and Jennifer, called Jen, was born fifteen months later. Lori basically retired to take care of the two babies. Bob was traveling a lot with increasing responsibilities, so she was often on her own with the house and the kids. While he worked incredibly hard to never miss a critical event in their lives and took red-eye flights to get home, it was necessary for Lori to be fully capable and independent.

She says, "Looking back on it, I was forced by circumstances to develop skills and attitudes that have served me and us well, especially now as I fight my disease."

Even though they always missed Bob, the kids and Lori were self-sufficient and hyperactive together. Aly says, "I remember going to yoga or exercise class with her. I remember that, even though I was very young. And I remember a lot of our Connecticut summers being mostly with her. We belonged to a country club, and she took us swimming there. What I think of the most was her just being a mom. There were times, because of my dad's job, that they also both traveled a lot together when we were younger, and of course that was hardest on a kid. But even when they went on these long trips, there were always surprises hidden around the house. Things scheduled for us to do—always. She has always been a scheduler, a planner, the ultimate caretaker. She still has her calendar with everything that is going on every day, just like a mom."

After the girls were in elementary school, she started a business with a female partner. They bought a six-acre piece of property and developed three houses on it. Her partner's husband was the contractor. Lori's father had dabbled in real estate, and she had observed him doing all the work. "I guess I was following his example. Life was, on balance, complex but rich."

Bob was also finding his way as a businessman. By age thirty-six he had risen to vice president of marketing services for his company and in 1978 was hired by GE Capital to be president of their insurance division, necessitating the family's move to Rhode Island.

In the town of Warwick, in a charming section called Cowesett, on a hill overlooking the East Greenwich Cove, they found an old house they both loved. It was what is known as a "honeymoon house." Here is how it got that interesting name. In the nineteenth century, captains would go to sea for years at a time, whaling or trading with the Far East. When they returned to Rhode Island with a substantial fortune, they would marry and take their brides to Europe. While they were abroad for their honeymoon, they would have their houses built, and hence the name. The Patins' old honeymoon house was beautiful but needed a lot of work. Restoring it was Lori's project. She hired the architect and the builders and supervised construction.

Then, nine years later, Bob got an even better offer to lead Washington National, a public diversified insurance and financial services company based in Evanston, a suburb of Chicago. After Bob checked out the company and was intrigued by the opportunity, he came home so he and Lori could talk to the children. Aly was a senior in high school at the time. They decided they couldn't possibly move because she had just gotten herself really established and was doing well. It would have been devastating to their daughter to have to start over in a new city at this critical time in her life.

The Patins decided she would stay with the girls in Cowesett, and Bob would work in Evanston during the week but fly home on weekends. The girls didn't find this arrangement much of a change from what they were used to. Aly said, "It didn't even seem like a full year. It was, but we were adjusting, and he was coming home pretty often." Actually, it seemed to Lori that he was home more often than before; at least she could predict when he would be home with more confidence—always the Friday afternoon flight from Chicago and the early Monday flight back. Three nights at home almost every week.

Aly, then off to Tulane, acknowledges that she was more of a handful for her mother than Jen: "I talked back. Jen is much more like my mom in that you don't give way to emotions, you just suck it up." Her first year in college, she had a hard time leaving home. Aly says, "Mother was very supportive of me and reassuring. And then I was the first daughter off to college, and I remember as a young kid, saying, 'You are going to go to college with me, right?' Like, 'I don't go by myself, right? You are coming with me?' And I was thinking, *I am never going to leave home ever.* Then college comes around and I was terribly homesick. But she kept in contact constantly. I always got wonderful things in the mail, very thoughtful, making sure to keep in touch."

Lori adds, "That bonding with Aly created a special relationship that endures to this day and is a critical element in my support system as I deal with my health challenge."

So with Aly headed for college and Jen a junior in high school, their parents anticipated that all the commuting would end as the school year finished. Jen and her mother would move to Chicago to be with Bob so she would finish high school there.

But it didn't quite work out that way. When Jen's junior year finished, she realized she didn't want to move to Chicago for her senior year either. She had become a really good field hockey player—number-one scorer in the state—and there wasn't a lot of field hockey in Chicago at that time. So they made the sacrifice and committed to her as they had to Aly, that she should have the opportunity to stay in Rhode Island for that all-important senior year. Bob agreed to commute for another year, living by himself in the apartment one block from work. Lori says, "It was no mean sacrifice on his part, either. Guys, despite their ability to hide it, get lonely too."

However, Jen actually loved that year alone with her mother before she went to college. She says, "Mom and I became really good friends during that time. My dad was home on weekends, but the rest of the time, it was just the two of us. We are such good friends now. I think it really was the beginning of creating that relationship for us."

Lori believes it is "a real, substantive relationship that sustains me, and hopefully her, just like my relationship with Aly. With life's challenges come marvelous blessings."

During the time Bob was commuting, Lori kept herself very busy. Because the nights were lonely after the girls went to bed, she decided to indulge in a hobby. She had always loved crafts, so she used free time at night to design needlepoint and cross-stitch pillows. During Christmas, demand was so steep that she sometimes stayed up almost all night to complete orders. "My days were full, so full that I got a mother's helper one day a week to give me some free time."

She taught aerobics and had already started what Bob called a "slum landlord" business even before Bob took his job in Chicago. She bought and fixed up small houses near the beach to rent to college students during the school year and then to families for the summer. In the weeks between student and summer rentals, she had to do a lot of fixing up, so she hired the girls to help. It was enormous fun for all of them. She paid them minimum wage, and the three ladies stood around in bathing suits, painting. "My life was frenetic, but it fed my needs and our situation."

But then one summer day, Lori noticed something odd. "I didn't think that much of it at the time, but I didn't forget it either. Aly, Jen, and I were slapping white paint on a beach rental home. Holding the can in one hand and the brush in the other, I suddenly felt the hand with the paint can start to shake uncontrollably. So much so I was worried I would splash paint. When I put the can down, my left hand stopped trembling. That was in 1987, twenty-five years ago." That was when Parkinson's first showed its ugly hand.

A little later that same summer when something similar happened, it seemed a little more ominous. Lori had gone to Florida to visit her widowed mother—she went almost every month for a few days. She noticed it when she was reading the paper in the morning, drinking coffee. She held the paper out in front so she could see both pages at once, and her whole arm would start quaking. She thought, *Oh what is this?* "My dad, interestingly enough, had a tremor in his hand too. Unfortunately, he never lived long enough for me to ask him much about it, but I remember mentioning it to him one time. I said, 'Your hands are shaking.' He said it was because of his heart medication, and it may have been; I don't know. Anyway, I put the paper down, and I never held it out like that to read again."

Parkinson's was incubating, lurking, if not already there, sending warning signals, getting ready to assert itself.

In 1991, the day after Jen graduated, the family moved to Chicago and soon started looking at houses. They weren't in any hurry to buy because Lori wanted to see everything. "By myself

I found the house we are living in now. This romantic English cottage perched high on a cliff overlooking Lake Michigan was just standing empty. It didn't even have a For Sale sign. We really wanted to live on the water, but houses like this are very difficult to find. I asked my Realtor what was the deal with this beautiful Tudor cottage, so obviously empty. She said, 'Oh, that house is in litigation. I guess the person who owned it tried to sell it under false pretenses. So there is escrow money at risk and lawsuits flying. You don't even want to get involved.' I told her, 'Maybe we do.' I hadn't even been inside yet." It had been empty so long—a couple of years—that it was the pits. It must have had the original kitchen from the 1920s. Its bathrooms were updated in the '40s, and it had only one and a half baths. "It would be a money pit. But we loved the idea of it, and it was right smack on Lake Michigan—and I could be the 'fixer'!"

So Bob found a lawyer specializing in working out litigious real estate deals, and with the help of the bank, put together an offer and told both parties that the Patins were interested in the house but only if they moved fast. He said, "Here is a cash deal with no contingencies. If you are interested in selling it, we want it now." Well, the two warring parties talked to each other a little bit and decided it wasn't such a bad deal, a lot better than continuing to pay mortgages and taxes and throwing away money on lawyers. Two weeks later they closed. "We had our home on the lake, and I had a project," Lori says.

"For the next year and a half, I made this house my job." Once work started, she served as the general contractor and was there working every day. Lori interviewed seven architects and seven builders until she found the ones she wanted, Steve Sider and Denis Smalley. It turned out they had worked together before. Sider, the architect, promised every room would have a view of the lake. "I didn't think it was possible, but he did it. Smalley did an excellent job of matching the fine 1920s craftsmanship. Our house had been built in '21 as a summer cottage for a family who lived in Chicago."

Lori and Bob lived in one bedroom upstairs for almost a year with all their stuff in boxes. It wasn't so bad at first. They expanded the kitchen and planned to add on a family room with the master bedroom and bath above. They went around to look for materials that would match the wood on the floors, stucco walls throughout, and stone, not brick, for this vintage house. Living with the construction was not ideal, but they could tolerate it until the contractors started tearing everything down for the addition. Soon the Patins realized they needed to move out until the addition was completed. Luckily a friend in Wilmette, a nearby suburb, asked if they would mind staying at her place for several weeks to mind her pool while she was on an extended vacation. It would prove a great break from sawdust and noise, but the contractors assured them that they'd need to be offsite longer so they had to find another place to live for a couple of months.

Lori and Bob took all their coupons and certificates for airlines and hotels accumulated from all those years of Bob's travel and used them to stay two months in the Renaissance Hotel. The funny thing is that the hotel had an absolutely, under-no-circumstances policy about taking dogs. So every night she took their dog up the elevator to the room, wrapping it in a blanket like a baby. "One ugly kid that barked in the elevator. We told other folks riding the elevator that the kid had a bad cough."

Back in 1995, when they moved into their completed home, the slate on the addition looked much newer than the roof on the rest of the house, but now it has grown worn and matches well. And Lori's gardens are mature now too, like her relationship with Parkinson's. "I do love my home that I helped create, and I do love my flowers. And I do hate my Parkinson's."

Even though her life was going so well, Lori was about to have to come to grips with the disease. In 1996, she had another strange experience that she didn't consider anything important until she got her diagnosis. Aly was living in Austria with her boyfriend. Her parents decided to visit them and go skiing together. Lori explains, "It was a gorgeous day, perfect conditions, and I love to ski, but every time I tried to turn left, I fell. I wrote it off to a bad binding or a faulty ski." Parkinson's had once again sent a signal that they still didn't know how to read. It was coming not to visit, but to stay.

The next year, Lori's quaking had grown so pronounced and so frequent that she couldn't ignore it any longer. She developed various techniques for controlling it. Whenever she did something with her left hand, the trembling stopped. It was always on her left side—her left hand, arm, and foot. "I could hold my hand to still the tremors. I got so I was holding it all the time. When I carried a coffee cup, I only filled it halfway so the coffee wouldn't spill. Still, I hated how the spoon rattled against the cup. I was afraid I was going to drop it. It was frightening. I knew this was not normal. I once said to Bob, 'This better not be Parkinson's.'"

They made an appointment with her internist, who recommended they see a movement disorders specialist, Dr. Michael Rezak, a nationally known Parkinson's expert. When Lori called Dr. Rezak's office, she was told he was booked solid for six months but she could see a part-time associate in the practice. She was desperate. She took any appointment she could get.

On December 17, 1997, after she had run some of the basic tests, Dr. Rezak's associate called Lori into her office. She said, "Sit down. I want to talk to you." She started crying when she said, "I have to tell you that I suspect you are right. You do have Parkinson's disease. I am so sorry." Lori says, "At this point I didn't even know what the diagnosis meant. But my first reaction was fear: I was scared for Bob. Not for me. I didn't know what he would do without me, and I was sure this was a death sentence, probably a quick one at that."

After Lori went home, she started to think about it and decided she did not feel comfortable working with an associate in a movement disorder medical practice with a diagnosis of this consequence. So she called her internist and explained the situation. He is a friend of Dr. Rezak's, so he called the office and got Lori in to see Dr. Rezak the next day. By this time, it was January. Dr. Rezak said he knew immediately that Lori had Parkinson's and gave her a prescription for a drug, Artane, to help modify the symptoms. He immediately tried to quell her fears about this being a death sentence. He said PD patients who take care of themselves and do all the right things—exercising, eating, taking their meds, and sleeping well—do well for years, sometimes decades.

Lori says, "What he did at that moment was give me a much more powerful drug than Artane: hope! Although I couldn't fully grasp what he was giving me at the time because I was still in shock, I would eventually start taking this more potent drug in large doses . . . and I still do."

Because she received the diagnosis so close to Christmas, she decided not to tell the girls immediately. "I didn't want to spoil their holiday. Then I decided to postpone telling them a little longer because in January we have several birthdays, and I didn't want to ruin those either. It was February, nearly Valentine's Day, when Bob and I told them. We asked Aly to meet us at Jen's house."

Aly remembers that conversation well, knowing it had to be something very serious. "It was only a couple of times in my life that I remember somebody asking me to sit down so they can tell you something. I knew it was going to be a devastating talk."

As her parents brought the news home to their daughters that day, Aly remembered that she had noticed that something was not right with her mother two years before she was diagnosed. Aly says, "Everything else was completely normal, but she had a slight tremor and slight shaking. I thought it was odd, but she was so healthy in every other aspect that I didn't really think about it. I did tell her, 'Mom, you might want to get that checked out, you might have some nerve thing going on.' But I never ever really believed it was something neurological." Today Aly is a nurse, but at that time she was just very interested in medicine, enough to know that she "was a little bit relieved that it was Parkinson's and not a tumor. I knew okay, this is survivable, as opposed to a brain tumor or terminal cancer. And then I thought, *Okay, well now we need to know where do we go from here.* Hearing about the diagnosis, thinking about my response to it then and thinking about it now after I know what it really means, I was scared then, but it is terrifying now."

Jen had also noticed her mother's arm shaking years before. Jen says, "But when I asked her about it, she said, 'Oh, it is just nothing.' As long as she was okay with it so was I. That is Mom. She doesn't like anyone to make a fuss over her." Jen was pregnant with her second child at the time when her mother and father told her that Lori had Parkinson's, and that colored her reaction. She adds, "I knew it was serious. You know, when she first told us, my sister clearly knew what it meant. She started sobbing, and then my mom started crying. I just sat there thinking, *What the heck is going on?* because I had never even heard of Parkinson's, and because I was still in 'baby world' at that time anyway."

Lori was still reeling from the diagnosis herself. In fact, she says, "I felt like I just wanted to sit in a corner and cry until I died. Then something powerful happened that reinforced what Dr. Rezak had told me, but I wasn't able to grasp at that first meeting." In March, she got an invitation to an American Parkinson's Association seminar in Chicago. She decided it would be a good idea to go because she could get additional information about case studies and drug trials.

"A neurologist at that APA symposium said something that day that changed my life: 'No one ever dies quickly from Parkinson's.' I was riveted. Suddenly I realized: I've got time. Dr. Rezak had already told me this, but I just couldn't hear it. I've got time! I don't have to let this disease control my life. Another doctor, another expert, just told me this is not going to kill me quickly. I can make the best of my life. I can choose to not let this get to me. And, if it does, then I can figure out another way to fight. And another way after that. I can beat this."

Then and there, Lori made a contract with Parkinson's disease: "You take your best shot, and I am going to do everything in my power to beat you. I'm not going to just use conventional medicine. I'll explore alternative treatments and physical therapy and anything else the experts or I can think of. I'll try anything that might make a difference, even if it doesn't pan out."

Fifteen years ago she thought she had about ten decent years left and she should experiment with anything that might help. Lori says, "As I look back, some things worked better than others, but I'm convinced that each of us is different and will respond differently to different therapies. Whatever it takes. I am buying time until research finds a cure."

When the Patins lived in Connecticut, they used to hike in the White Mountains in New Hampshire. In those days Lori had such good balance that she ran down the mountain, literally skipping from stone to stone. "I cannot do that anymore, but I am doing something better. Life handed me a mountain, and I am climbing back up."

CHAPTER 2

The Crisis

Courage doesn't always roar. Sometimes courage is the quiet voice at the end of the day, saying, "I will try again tomorrow."[1]

THE SUMMER OF 2011 WAS a turning point for Lori. She lapsed into a coma twice. When her brother, Don, surprised her by visiting her in intensive care, she thought, *I must be dying. Why else would my brother be here?* When she went into rehab, she wondered, *Will I ever be able to live at home again?* For a while, it looked as though she would have to renege on her contract to beat Parkinson's disease. Then she dug in deeper. Somehow, with a combination of support from so many, Lori tapped whatever reserves were still left and started over. She went back to her old tactics and began adding new ones. Since waking out of those comas, her progress has been steady, and once again she is able to do things she couldn't do for years. This fall, 2013, she is not only living at home but is horsing around with her four-year-old grandson and practicing tai chi, even back to taking dancing lessons. She doesn't have tremors anymore. It is a miracle. Her neurologist, Dr. Rezak, says he has never seen such an improvement in a Parkinson's patient and knows of nothing else like it in the literature.

---

[1]   Mary Anne Radmacher and Jonathan Lockwood Huie, *Simply an Inspired Life* (San Francisco: Red Wheel/Weiser, 2009), 177.

That terrible summer, Lori often had to lie down because she had such a hard time catching her breath. Her blood pressure went really low, down to 70/50, partly because the meds she takes slow everything down and partly because that's a side effect of the disease. Today it is much better at 110/60—still on the low side but acceptable. Her weight dropped to 94 pounds. She says, "I looked awful and felt worse. People still call me thin even though I now weigh 112, but I don't feel thin because I am so much more substantial than I was. I fill out my clothes. I look like the woman I once was. It's a thrill to be able to wear the things I wore when I was fully me. My boobs grew back—which Bob is really excited about, the horny devil!"

Before her turnaround, she felt terrible that she couldn't be the kind of grandmother to Aly's son, Matthew, as she was to Jen's children when they were the same age. Lori says, "I longed to pick him up and walk around rocking him. Still, I felt so happy just sitting by his crib and watching him sleep."

Before she went into the hospital, something happened that amused her but gave her family great concern. Lori explains: "One funny thing was that I started having hallucinations. I know that sounds really quite odd that I find those funny, and my family certainly was not laughing, but I wasn't scared at all. I would get to talk to my father who has been dead for years, or to my brother, who lives in Ohio. Or I would see lots of animals—dogs, coyotes, even a zebra. Once I told Aly that she was in the living room delousing a zebra. You have to laugh at that one. These hallucinations weren't transparent; they had form and shape and were as three-dimensional as you or I. They didn't scare me because I knew they were hallucinations, partly because it wasn't logical to have my dead father in the family room or a zebra in the living room and partly because I just knew it was not real."

In February 2011, the doctors put in a pacemaker for her heart. That was supposed to help with her blood pressure, and mostly it has been a success.

In June, when the crisis hit, all Lori's doctors collaborated under Dr. Rezak's supervision to slightly reduce her meds in the hopes that a more simplified formula might be absorbed better by her system. As soon as she came out of the second coma, she started to recover. Progress was slow, but progress was good nevertheless. She was up and walking by the end of the first day. She had to use a walker, but still—what an improvement over lying in bed for weeks. Bob and Lori did laps around the halls of the rehab center all hours of the day and night. She got rid of the walker as soon as she was able because she could not tolerate needing mechanical help to walk.

Although Dr. Rezak can't confirm this, Lori's theory is the comas were "my body's way of trying to heal itself, like computer software rebooting. I think I wasn't able to fully heal while I was awake, so my body shut down into a deep sleep because the body supposedly fixes itself while you sleep." The type of coma she went into is called a "spindle coma," or an "altered sleep state coma," so it makes sense that it offered some of the same benefits as a deep sleep.

She says, "While this is just personal guesswork, coming up with a theory about what is happening to me is a really important part of my healing process because a lot of fighting this disease is about trying to make sense out of the unknown. If I believe my body knows what to do to help heal itself, even in a primitive, subconscious way, then I have some control or at least some influence over outcomes. Any suggestion that I have no role is unacceptable because it would turn me into a helpless victim." Instead, she is under contract to battle this disease. When one plan doesn't work, she will have to come up with a new plan.

Lori doesn't really like to talk about herself, especially about things that are either not so positive or seem like "I am any kind of special, which I'm not." So she is going to let her family and some close friends, Anne and Tom Heynen and Judy and Tom Hamilton, explain how she got to the crisis of the summer of 2011 and her remission since.

First, let's allow her to speak.

Lori

When I visited Dr. Rezak three months after I came home and he told me he had never seen anyone with Parkinson's get better the way I have, Bob asked me, "How does that make you feel?" I responded, "It only increases my conviction that God wants me to do something with this." Even though I am a very private person and hate talking about myself, I want to take the risk of sharing my story to offer help to others who are struggling with something equally challenging in their lives. Trust me; I know myself. If I—with all the normal human flaws and weaknesses I own—can fight my fight and make some headway against something truly ugly, so can you.

Bob

I am really glad Lori is letting us have a crack at explaining what happened last summer. For one thing, she slept through a lot of it and doesn't even know how awful it was. For another, it is part of her positive attitude that she never dwells on the bad things that have happened to her. If you heard only her story, you would never know how bad it got so you wouldn't be able to appreciate how good she is now. So, please bear with us while her friends and family tell you how much Lori means to us, how frightened we were, and how proud we are now. Because we love her so, we have all lived her struggle. When someone you love has an incurable and irreversible disease, so do you. You either fight it together, or it will eat you both independently.

We were doing okay for quite a while, but in 2011, it became clear the Parkinson's was advancing more rapidly until it was getting the upper hand. Lori got so bad that she went into the intensive care unit at Evanston Hospital from June 12 to 20 and from the hospital to the Mather Pavilion Skilled Nursing Residence from June 30 to July 31.

But let me back up to set a context for this part of her story. We had been seeing Parkinson's slow, relentless progress for years despite all Lori's best efforts to attack it on every front. As it progressed, we tried to figure out how to strategically position ourselves so that she could get the best possible care. During the first nine or ten years after her diagnosis, I still needed to work. When in 1999 I started working for CNA, a large public insurance company, I cut a three-year deal because I didn't know how long Lori could go without my help. By 2003 I packed it in. She was declining at such a rate that I knew I couldn't continue to work full time since I wanted to be her primary caretaker. This decision took no great soul-searching on my part. She'd taken care of me all these years; it is simply my turn. Now it is time to at least try to pay back what she'd done for me in so many ways for so long.

We've had our darker moments, but the darkest moment was last summer.

Lori dropped to ninety-four pounds. She fell all the time. Whenever she walked, I had to hold on to her to keep her steady. She was having massive hallucinations. I interpret what happened as a negatively reinforcing cycle where one bad thing causes another bad thing to happen. She didn't feel good, so sometimes she forgot to take her meds. This caused her to stop exercising and hydrating, which made her feel worse, so the whole cycle spiraled downward. She got to the point where she couldn't shoulder the burden any longer. Then they hospitalized her—the nadir of her negative spiral, though we didn't know it at the time.

I have always tried to go into every personal or business battle armed with the logic that says, "We are going to figure this out. We will do whatever the situation calls for." But this time I was truly not sure what the next phase would be. For the first time I had to confront the ugly possibility that Lori might not be coming home.

When she went into the coma, that was the worst. When your partner won't come to life, won't acknowledge who you are, won't respond to your requests, you die inside. And when the doctors can't provide answers, you damn near panic.

I am pretty good at reality, so I said to myself, "This is it." And I started to make plans for the worst-case scenario, even though I didn't really want to believe it. I knew Lori was a fighter like no other. And I think I am reasonably tough, but I am nothing compared to her. Still, I started to live with the conclusion that even the toughest can finally be worn down when life's blows are so constant and so severe.

After she woke from the comas, the experts all said, "We don't know exactly what to make of this"—not exactly confidence inspiring. When she left the hospital to go into rehab, her doctor said, "She will do rehab, and then we will see how she comes out of rehab and where that takes us." In other words, the experts knew just about as much as we did, maybe less considering they couldn't factor in what her mental and emotional state would be and if her usual tenacity would kick back in. Needing to make a plan, I began to research assisted-living facilities by talking to people about where their parents lived. The trick would be to find a place that didn't look like an admission that her situation was hopeless. That would have killed her.

Suddenly things took a turn for the better. She started to do really well in rehab. *Maybe there's hope!* I thought. The doctors had reduced her meds a little bit, and there could have been some trigger in that former combination of meds that was not helping. It was probably exacerbated by dehydration. So she gained strength, drank gallons of liquids, ate hearty meals, and put on weight. No more hallucinations—they had scared the crap out of us. Her attitude was better. Actually, her attitude bounced back remarkably. I think when she first went into rehab, she thought she might never come out, and that thought got her dander up. There's something deeply embedded in the girl so that near defeat calls forth another charge up the hill. I now think that the soldier, rested and renewed, wanted to get back into the battle.

Coming home gave her a huge psychological lift. She got right back to the things that she had been doing before, all the good things with diet, exercise, sleep, and treatments that she had dropped when she got into that negative spiral. Now she is not only better than last summer but is probably better than she was years ago. We're gonna ride the good tide without any assumptions about how long it lasts. We'll revel in the time we've got and make every moment count.

Nevertheless, I know there will be further battles with the disease, and that really pisses me off. The very idea that something can attack someone you love so relentlessly seems just unfair. Sometimes, I think, *Dear God, take this away,* knowing that having this disappear through that kind of intercession is a long shot even though her God will always be near to her.

What I do know somewhere deep in my soul is that I can face whatever we have to face if we do it together. Lori is the best hero I know and an inspiration to us all. She never gives up hope. She has learned that life rewards those who show courage with hope. Ever hopeful, ever learning, ever resourceful, she lives life to the fullest and keeps finding new ways to fight the great fight. I would never want to be her opponent.

Jen

My mother is not only better than she was last summer, she is better now than she was ten years ago. Her balance and strength are so much better. She doesn't fall anymore. She was very fragile. She doesn't seem like that to me anymore. So when I say better, I mean in many ways. She has put on more weight too. She was just rail thin.

But last summer things got really terrible. She started having breathing problems to the point where she was actually passing out. And that is when my dad started taking her regularly to the emergency room.

Also, Mom was seeing things that weren't there. She started seeing people in the room and actually talked to people who weren't there. You could tell that she'd think she saw somebody because she would make a comment about that person. I would say, "What are you talking about?" She would say, "Why is Aunt

Jeanette sitting in the living room?" I would say, "Aunt Jeanette is in Ohio; she is not here." So she would say, "Oh, I know. I am just kidding around." She was trying to cover up, which we all knew, but you can imagine how that scared us.

That awful summer she also started becoming very forgetful and confused. I would tell her something and then she would ask me the same question not too long after. Then I would say, "We just talked about that, remember?" She would say, "Oh, that's right, that's right."

We thought, *She has kept this disease at bay for so long, maybe this is a turning point. Maybe it is all catching up to her.* Between the low blood pressure, the breathing issues, and the hallucinations, nobody knew what was going on. They did every test in the book. The experts never came up with any conclusive answer—which was enormously frustrating.

Now she is back to doing all her stuff. She has started over and again is pushing herself. That is the reason she is doing so well right now. It is both a blessing and a curse, in the sense that she's winning most of the battles, but she sometimes tires herself out.

And then in August, we had another big problem; not my mom this time. My dad went into the hospital just a few weeks after Mom came home from rehab. When it started raining during a beach party they gave for their church, he went running down the slippery stairs to check on the boat and fell and broke three ribs. With broken ribs, the doctors in the emergency room told him, "There is nothing really that you can do except wait." He came home but soon got really, really sick and kept vomiting. So Dad went back to the hospital to discover that he had diverticulitis. The ribs had punched a hole in his colon, exposing the disease. Although they initially solved the problem with antibiotics, he eventually had to have surgery to repair it. You would never have known that he was suffering because he was so focused on her.

An important lesson we all learned from the situation, however, is the value of my mother's caregivers. My dad is her most important caregiver, but she has many others, so she got along fine while he was in the hospital. We've come to have enormous respect for everyone who's in our mother's circle of care.

Aly

Today Mom is worlds better, not just better than the terrible summer of 2011 but better than she was in 2001 at my wedding. Anybody who sees her, who knows how she was before, is astonished. When we had an engagement party for someone in my husband's family last fall, just about everyone there knew how horrible the situation had been six months prior. As soon as she walked into the party, everyone in my husband's family said, "Oh my God, we didn't even recognize your mom. Wow." While she was dancing at the wedding, people applauded.

When Mom was diagnosed, I was twenty-six years old. I have a distinct picture of Mom's condition four years later because that is when I got married. Her deterioration over that short time was significant. In 1997 when she got her diagnosis, her balance seemed fine and so was her gait. The only visible evidence of her Parkinson's was a slight tremor. But at my wedding in 2001, Mom had so many tremors and such a hard time keeping her balance that you could see she was having trouble walking down the aisle. I have a clear mental image of Dad helping and guiding her, keeping her straight. In the middle of the ceremony I just stopped and watched. I knew at that point the PD was taking its toll.

Even though she wasn't the active, healthy Mom I grew up with, mostly the progress of her Parkinson's had been slow. She worked so hard at keeping it at bay that she was, in many ways, doing okay with it. I didn't notice any big dramatic change until the last three years. These years stand out for me because my son, Matthew, was three, so they were big years for me. I remember being scared to let her hold him as a newborn. Now she picks him up with ease. So that is another milestone marking my growing awareness of how far she has come back from where PD had taken her.

Just to show you how strong and stubborn my mother is, let me tell you about something that happened a number of years ago when her Parkinson's was still relatively mild. While visiting her aging mother in Florida, she ran across a street and tripped, shattering her hand and wrist. Although she did go to the emergency room and have a cast put on it, she was determined not to have any surgery done until she returned home two weeks later, even after X-rays confirmed massive damage. She simply wasn't willing to give up caring for her mother to have her own problem fixed. When she returned to Chicago, her hand and wrist had to be completely rebuilt by a top hand surgeon, Tom Wiedrich, a good friend who told her that if it she'd waited any longer she would have had permanent damage. Mom put her own mother first. The woman has priorities!

Four years ago, Mom started having such difficulty breathing that she would faint and fall down. The following year it got so bad that she would have to stop at the top of the stairs to catch her breath. Then a couple of times she was incontinent because she had what seemed like minor seizures. Once while I was staying with her because Dad was out of town, it was harder to take care of her than my year-old baby because she kept fainting. Every time she fell, I took her pulse. It would be around thirty—half a healthy pulse rate. When my Dad came home, I told him, "I don't care how many people said that she doesn't need a pacemaker; she needs to be reevaluated." Finally they determined that the breathing issues stemmed at least partly from her very, very slow heart rate, one of the side effects of the medicine she takes for her PD. Once she got the pacemaker in February 2011, she got so much better. Again we realized how complex health issues can be and how integrated the care needs to be to stay on top of an evolving situation—and how resolute the patient has to be to consistently consider new options for new situations.

Even so, it got to the point where every time I answered the phone and heard my dad's voice, I would think, *Oh my God*, because he had called so many times to tell me, "Your mother is back in the emergency room." Two years ago, she fell in the garage and literally broke the drywall with her head. I remember getting that phone call at work: "Your mom is in the ER. They are working her up for a bleed, a head bleed." Being a nurse in intensive care, I deal with this all the time at work, but it is a lot different when it happens to your mother. I kept thinking, *Oh my God, this can't be real.* That is when I thought, *Something has got to change.*

And it did change—for the worse. The worst was last year, when Matt and I were in Mexico celebrating our ten-year wedding anniversary. That was the summer of 2011. Dad called to say, "Your mom is in the intensive care unit. She is in a coma." Since she was at my sister hospital in the ICU, the hospitals are close enough that I could call to talk to the physician and the charge nurse there. For me, as a nurse, hearing "coma" and not being able to see her until I could get back from Mexico was terrible. I had in my mind the nursing concept of a typical coma—not that any are typical—which is a little different than the altered sleep state coma that was her actual condition. The more research I did and the more people I talked to, the more I came to figure out that she was basically stuck in the sleep state. I had never heard of this before. I thought, *This is really scary. Now where do we go from here?*

But the altered sleep state coma didn't come out of nowhere. She slid into it gradually. Several times just prior to the coma, Dad couldn't make Mom wake up. He would call and say, "I can't wake her up, Aly. She has been sleeping until noon. I don't know what's going on." I would tell him to call the doctor. She would be fine for a few days, but then it would happen again. When she went into the comas in the hospital, we really couldn't wake her. Not us. Not the docs. Not Dad. No one. While the comas only lasted for a day or so each time, the uncertainty was terrifying. No one had an answer about why they had occurred or what to do for them.

Terrible as it seemed at the time, the coma was the start of something good: Parkinson's reversal. When Mom came out of it, she started to get better immediately and kept improving to the point where today she has no tremors; her balance is much better, and so is her gait; she is full of energy and playing with Matthew again. Thank God.

Now that we have come out on the good side, I think that whole ordeal was probably one of the best things that could have happened because it forced her to give up some control. I really think that is why she has gotten so much better. Because she had to go into the Mather Pavilion for rehab after coming out of the comas, she had to put herself under the control of the staff there. She was forced to allow others to help.

At the Mather, they helped her get control over another big problem: her meds. One of the things with Parkinson's medications is that they have to absolutely be taken within a half-hour window of time. There can't be any monkeying around. You can't take two later to make up for missing a dose, especially when you are having short-term memory loss; this can be a problem. In rehab, we figured out that Mom was still in charge of her medications. Sometimes she would forget; other times she would double up. This was not helping her at all. Once she got into the nursing home, it was all taken out of her hands. She was put on a very strict regimen where her medications were doled out on schedule. Now my dad is in charge of her meds, a job he actually enjoys as it gives him comfort that the right meds are in her system at the right time and in the right doses. It also helps him sleep better, and that's good. He likes being in charge since he's a bit of a control freak.

The nursing home not only took charge of her medicine but of her food intake as well. I had never seen my mother as thin as she was when she came to Mather. She didn't seem to be the vibrant, strong, don't-mess-with-me woman I had grown up with. At the Mather, they put an end to that by feeding her six meals a day, including snacks. They were feeding her all the time so she gained a healthy amount of weight. She was getting stronger every day as well, thanks to her exercise routines, provided by caring therapists who didn't put up with any slacking off. Tough love for a tough lady. Very soon we could see a rebound underway that gave us far more hope than we'd had for quite a while.

I couldn't be more grateful to the people at rehab because they forced her to really take care of herself. For once, Mom was in a place where she couldn't think about anybody else. For a good three weeks to a month, it was just all out of her hands, so she was forced to actually focus on caring for herself. She couldn't even try to take care of my dad, the dog, or the house. She came home steadier, stronger, and beefed up. It got her started on a really good routine that she has carried on at home.

Of course when she came home, we had a bad surprise as Dad ended up in the hospital after he fell and broke his ribs.

Dad also recently finished radiation treatment for prostate cancer, so it's not like she's the only one we need to worry about. But you will never hear him talk about himself. He insists that it's not about him. It's about her and the people who love her. He's her partner in this fight, but she's the only one who can win this battle.

Tom and Judy Hamilton

Tom: Judy and I have known Lori and Bob a long time. I am involved at church and they are too. I met them at a meeting at church late at night. Bob had just come in covered in paint because he and Lori had been painting one of the apartments.

Judy: She has had an amazing turnaround. It is like night and day. It has made Bob very happy. Here she is, doing better than ever. I know Lori thought, *Well, I will be in a nursing home the rest of my life.*

Tom: We all thought that.

Judy: I didn't. She was determined that she was going to come home.

Tom: Even through the worst crises of last summer, there is no drama with Bob and Lori. There is no drama in anything that they do for each other. No drama, no horns blaring. I think this has the effect on minimizing the impact of the disease.

For example, Bob is the only man I know who goes into the ladies' room. If Lori takes too long in there, Bob goes in and finds her. I have seen him do that several times, and he does it in such a way that there is no commotion, no focus on him. Not only is it not blown out of proportion, it isn't even noticed. He does it with such confidence that there is no other agenda. Nobody is upset about a man in the ladies' room because he does it in such a caring fashion for Lori.

Judy: Speaking of the ladies' room, I remember an episode when we were at church and I took her there. On the way back she couldn't breathe and had to lie face down on the floor to stop and catch her breath. I was about to panic and was going to run and get Bob. I said, "Should I call an ambulance? Should I call and get some help?" Lori insisted, "No, no, you stay right here." She stayed very clear and rational, and then she was okay.

Tom: And so, Lori never lost her cool. She never lost her focus, never lost her perspective despite what she had been through already. Last summer when she was in the hospital, Bob would take his papers with him and sit out in the hallway working. All the while, Lori was lying unconscious in the ICU.

Bob never got upset. In his own take-charge way, with no drama, no superlatives, no adjectives, nothing like that, he would tell the staff at the Mather, "You've got to do this; you've got to do that." He had taken over her feeding, and then he took over her care. While she was in the hospital, Bob was in the process of either arranging for a facility where she could live or possibly making some major changes at the house so she could come home.

Judy: But Lori was determined. She had set her mind to meeting the milestones that the rehab program had set up. In order to go home, she had to reach certain weight milestones. She had to be able to get out of a chair by herself and stand up by herself before she could go home. And she did it.

Tom: Through all their trials, Bob knows implicitly that "I will be there for her," and so does Lori. Lori knows Bob will never ask too much of her, and Bob knows Lori will never ask too much of herself. He knows she will always be the best she can. There is never any hesitation for them. It is their life.

Anne and Tom Heynen

Anne: We have been friends with the Patins since before Lori was diagnosed. I recall watching Lori and Bob dance at an anniversary party in 1993 or '94 and thinking, *They are really good.* They didn't dance with other people, just together. Even then you could see a genuine bond between them. I think part of her success story has to do with the fact that they have such a strong bond and are so committed to each other.

The Holy Spirit was at work in Lori's turnaround. Last summer when she was in a coma, I thought she was going to die. To tell you the truth, lately I haven't even offered her my arm because she is walking so well and has virtually no tremors. I like to talk more about the positive than the negative because it has been such a success story.

Tom: Lori started taking golf lessons five years ago, long after she already had been diagnosed with the disease, a big step for somebody who has Parkinson's. She tried very hard, but it was almost pathetic to watch. It hurt to see her struggle so. Then of course she did not play at all for several years.

Last summer, one year after she got out of rehab, the four of us played golf. After Lori had that crisis last summer, we expected her to play much worse. In fact, we thought she would never play again. What a delightful surprise to see Lori hitting the ball about one hundred yards. She did have a problem putting, but she said she was going to take a lesson to improve. She wants to be as normal as normal can be and doesn't want you to feel sorry for her at all.

I want to give you an example of how resourceful and positive Lori is. We are in the Shawl Ministry together at Holy Comforter Church, where every week a group of ladies gets together to knit shawls for the sick and the poor. Up until last summer she continued to come even though she was having trouble knitting. In the entire hour and a half, she struggled to knit only one row. Before she came down with PD, she had knit beautiful, intricate garments. Still, she would smile and say, "I am not going to give up on the Shawl Ministry," even though she couldn't knit anymore. So she found another way to make shawls. She was ingenious enough to figure out a way to make a pretty shawl by tearing felt. After a while, some of the rest of us started making felt shawls too. Now she is back, smiling, and a big part of the group. And this Christmas our group made twenty of these great-looking shawls for the homeless.

After Bob and her daughters said she couldn't drive the car anymore, I took her places she wanted to go. Just getting out of the car was a struggle. As her condition got worse, I would help her out of the car, but she got so pigeon-toed and bent over that I would think, *I don't know how she can walk.*

Last year, her health took a nosedive. In May or June 2011, we went on our annual trip together, and I was alarmed by her deterioration. She was sitting at the table bent over like a jackknife. She could barely bring the fork to her mouth because her hands were shaking so badly. She looked frighteningly thin.

Tom: Leading up to the crisis, she just couldn't catch her breath. She'd have to sit down wherever she was. The Patins and the Heynens have tickets together for the Northwestern University football games. Twice when we were at a game, she had to sit down suddenly because she couldn't breathe. But it got even worse when she started having frequent fainting spells. Once she fell in the ladies' room and couldn't get up off the floor, and no one could help her at first because she was locked in the stall.

Anne: Lori can make something positive out of any experience. When she went into the Mather after she left the hospital, within a week, she knew all the people on her floor, as well as the nurses. When she was up and around a little bit more, I had lunch with her twice. I hadn't known her except in a friendship, but to see her in that environment changed my opinion of her. Some people would just stay in their room because they didn't want to be in rehab. Not Lori. She didn't complain about being there; she made the best of it. She made friends. She adopted other patients.

Lori told me, "People want to know what I did to get better. How *did* you do it? It is not because of any one thing. It is because of a commitment to do many things. It requires your ability to stay with it and not give up, and it is not easy."

She has been an inspiration to me.

CHAPTER 3

·········· ❦ ··········

Medicine

LORI PATIN HAS MADE A personal contract to fight to the death against Parkinson's. According to the terms of her contract, her efforts unite within a wheel grinding down on the disease. Every spoke contributes to the crushing power of the rim and fulfills a vital role in her campaign to live a full, normal, and healthy life. This wheel has five different spokes: medicine; friends and family; caregivers; exercise, diet, and sleep; and attitude and spirituality. Although they are all roughly equally important, let's start with medicine. It was within the world of medicine that Lori received the diagnosis that gave a name to her symptoms and a narrative about what to expect as the disease progressed. Although she has explored other medications and therapies, Western medicine offers the most effective way to treat Parkinson's symptoms. And medical research holds out the best hope for a cure. All that she does, all the medication, therapies, and treatments she takes are buying time until that research comes through with a cure for everyone with Parkinson's.

Lori

How did Bob and I feel when we first got the diagnosis? It was awful to hear that I had Parkinson's, but it was still so much better to know than not to know. Of course we had realized something was wrong for quite a while. Once we had the diagnosis, we could name the enemy and take action against it. As Bob says, "Data and reality are better than a vacuum or amnesia." It was tough, but it wasn't as if I had a diagnosis of terminal cancer.

Right at the outset, I enlisted one of the very best medical advisers in Chicago, one of the best Parkinson's specialists in the country, Michael Rezak, MD, PhD. Dr. Rezak used to practice at Evanston Hospital in Illinois. A few years ago, he was hired away by Central DuPage Hospital where he is medical director of the Movement Disorders Center and of the Movement Disorders Functional Neurosurgery Program at the Neurosciences Institute. Even though his new office is far less convenient than his former office, now more than an hour's drive rather than twenty minutes', there was no question that we would continue to see Dr. Rezak. He holds many state and regional positions in organizations fighting Parkinson's, such as medical director for the American Parkinson's Disease Association's National Young Onset Center and medical director for the Parkinson's Disease Research Society. He is so well respected that he is asked to speak at seminars across the country in order to give Parkinson's patients the most up-to-date and accurate information about their disease. My daughter Aly is a nurse in the ICU at Evanston Hospital where Dr. Rezak used to practice before he was stolen away by Central DuPage Hospital. Her opinion means more to me than almost anyone's, and she says Dr. Rezak is "the premier Parkinson's specialist in the Midwest." I knew he was the best on my first visit, when he gave me his cell phone number and said, "Call me anytime." Very few doctors do that anymore.

One of the first questions we asked Dr. Rezak was how long it would take the disease to evolve to its worst stage and death. Answer: in most cases, many years. It is not immediate. It is a chronic condition. That sounded good at first. But later-stage chronic is awful. You "freeze" and can't move. You have trouble swallowing. Your voice becomes a whisper. You can become depressed. There will likely come a point where you wish it would be over soon. As they say, Parkinson's doesn't kill you quickly; it kills you slowly and not kindly at the end. But I refused to accept that then as I do today. Per our contract, it's Parkinson's or me: one of us is going to lose, and I'll do my damnedest to make sure it isn't me.

As I told you in chapter 1, when Dr. Rezak took me on as a patient, he did a few simple tests that he continues to do every six months or so when I visit his office. I extend my arm out straight, and he has me turn it like a clock while he holds it. When I get to six o'clock, if I can keep it up at the same place for a couple of seconds, that means my Parkinson's is being held somewhat at bay. While I turn it, he can feel a cog, a kind of bump, at certain places during the turn. He said at that initial exam that he could feel a cog on the left side, but not the right—an indication that PD was attacking me on the left side. He does another test out in the hallway. I stand up and then he pushes me. I don't know when he's going to do it. How quickly I am able to catch myself lets him know how my balance is doing. In the last year, I have shown significant improvement in both tests. I practice them at home when I do my weight workout or practice tai chi.

Dr. Rezak says, "The balance problems are not that you feel wobbly or anything. I like to make the analogy that if you throw a cat up in the air, it will land on all fours. Humans have that same reflex hardwired into our nervous system. If somebody pushes you, you bring yourself back automatically. In Parkinson's, if you have what they call the 'postural reflex impairment,' when somebody pushes you, you just keep going. You can't catch yourself. Or, if someone pulls you backward, you start tumbling because you can't stop yourself. That is the kind of balance problem I am talking about. And not everybody with Parkinson's gets that. What we do in the office is, I come from behind and say, 'I want you to stop within one or two steps.' Then I pull her backward. If she takes more than two steps to catch herself, that's not normal. Physical therapy can help a little bit, but it is the decrease in this hardwired reflex that we are worried about."

What's been somewhat funny about the balancing tests Dr. Rezak does is that they are nothing compared to what Bob does to me at home. It's like his chance to "reward" me for all the little things I've done to irritate him over the years. We do the balancing exercises, but he does it in his own sadistic way! It's about his favorite game. He'll not only pull me back but also push me forward by surprise. He also likes to shove me sideways without warning, always within easy range of grabbing me if I'm going to fall. But Bob does it for much longer than the exam at Dr. Rezak's. He says he's just enhancing my balancing by repetitive activities that have nothing to do with any sort of "payback." I'll teach him about payback some night when he's sleeping!

Dr. Rezak is just plain amazed at how much I have improved. He says he may even write me up as a case study. He says, "I don't think we can explain it very well. It is very atypical. I think it is a combination of things. Of course, a key part is that Lori is very strong willed. She does all the right things for herself in terms of exercise and nutrition. Lots of my patients don't. In my practice, the people who exercise, who go to physical therapy, need less medicine. Their symptoms are milder. They are just better for longer periods of time."

Exercise is an ally I can call on at will. You can imagine the encouragement these words give to someone like me who remembers when she taught aerobics! This is something I can intellectually and emotionally own that can improve my situation. I do notice that when I exercise regularly, my symptoms are less pronounced. This makes me feel as if I have some kind of control over this disease, even if it is somewhat illusionary.

By way of an analogy, I've always loved the story about Chicken Little, and I think it has relevance to this aspect of me versus Parkinson's. This silly chicken is lying on his back in the middle of the road with his feet up in the air when someone comes along and asks him why he's doing it. He says, "The sky is falling." And the other one says, "So if that's true, what are you doing on your back with your feet up in the air?" He responds, "Well, one does what one can." Though I hope my efforts are more rational than Chicken Little's, I'm doing whatever I can to keep the Parkinson's sky from falling on me.

Dr. Rezak continues. "I think the exercise and nutrition, all those things she does have helped her, but Parkinson's does not reverse itself. Symptoms can wax and wane, but the disease in the brain itself does not reverse. She still has some symptoms, but she has gotten better, much better. We can slow things down sometimes with exercise and certain medications. Sometimes there are other things that might be exacerbating the symptoms. But those stressors—stress of any kind, physical or mental—can make her Parkinson's symptoms worse. So you know, if somehow we relieved the stressors that we hadn't recognized, that would help her symptoms get better. We don't look a gift horse in the mouth. We are very happy that she's had a big, huge turnaround."

One of the key things Dr. Rezak does for me is prescribe medication to control my symptoms. For all Parkinson's patients, getting medication right involves quite a bit of trial and error. Tailoring my medications is as much an art as a science. Dr. Rezak says he "micromanages" it. I started out taking Artane, a relatively mild pharmaceutical, to help control my tremors. It worked well enough, but because I hate taking medication of any kind I sought out alternative treatments. So I went to a holistic doctor who gave me herbs. The herbs worked for a year or so, and I thought they enhanced my Parkinson's medications. But I could tell Parkinson's was still there, lurking, ready to strike. I also took liquids, essences of flowers that were prescribed by another alternative practitioner. Both therapies were helpful to a degree because they seemed to keep my system clean, healthy, and receptive, ready for whatever life would deal out. But I knew I needed better weapons to take on a tough foe like PD, so I went back to Dr. Rezak's prescription. Now I am taking a battery of medications to combat my symptoms: Carbidopa-Levodopa (commonly known as L-Dopa), Pramipexole (a dopamine agonist), Pyridostigmine Symmetral (an antiviral agent), and Azilect (a MAO-B inhibitor). I also take a number of vitamin supplements to help keep my system supported.

I was willing to accept that Western medicine was part of the answer, but I needed to experiment with less-proven therapies as well. I didn't want to discount anything that might help. What I didn't understand then as well as I do now is that anything you put into your body can and will interact with everything else you put into your body, and sometimes there are side effects from the combination that can potentially make things worse. I got lucky with my early experiments and will continue to look at alternative approaches, but not without researching, as best I can, potential side effects. Life is complicated. A disease makes it more so.

As my disease progressed, about five years ago, Dr. Rezak put me on L-Dopa. L-Dopa can be a life changer not only because of its benefits but also because of its potential side effects such as diarrhea, loss of appetite, sleeping troubles, and severe motor fluctuations, so I resisted taking it for many months. L-Dopa is the organic precursor to dopamine, a neurotransmitter—in other words, a chemical released by nerve cells to send messages to other nerve cells. Parkinson's patients have a shortage of dopamine because the disease kills the cells in the brain that make this critical neurotransmitter.

When L-Dopa was discovered in the 1950s, it revolutionized the treatment of Parkinson's because it was the first drug to relieve the disease's symptoms. Ingesting straight dopamine would be ineffective because the drug is unable to cross the blood-brain barrier. But L-Dopa has the ability to cross the barrier into the brain where it will turn into dopamine. L-Dopa is always given in combination with another drug, carbidopa, which blocks L-Dopa from being metabolized in the gut, thus allowing more of it to reach the brain. All this is good, but L-Dopa is a very strong drug that can have some unpleasant side effects that are so bad I didn't like to take it. So I decided to fight the disease with my own body chemistry as long as I could. And here was where I had great intentions but made some decisions that came back to haunt me, even to the point of seriously threatening my marriage. Also, I was afraid that if I took the meds that Rezak recommended, they would wear off too quickly and then I would be forced to double up. Later I would have to double up again until eventually they wouldn't help me at all.

Dr. Rezak

I disagree with Lori: Parkinson's medicine doesn't wear off. If you need more medicine with Parkinson's, it is not like a narcotic where all of a sudden the same dose is not holding it. If you need more medicine, it is because the disease is progressing; your symptoms are getting worse. That's why you need more medicine. It isn't because you have taken the medicine for X amount of time and then it is no longer effective; it doesn't work that way. Lori isn't the only one to have that misconception; it is very common. It is just wrong to think, *I don't want to get started on it because I won't have it when I need it.* That's not the way L-Dopa works. Basically what we are doing is trying to replace dopamine in the brain where it has been depleted by the disease so you can use it there. It is just like diabetes, where you need to ingest the insulin because your body doesn't make enough.

Lori resisted taking her meds. But I think the fact that she wasn't willing to take her medicine, to take any medicine, is an indication that she wasn't totally accepting her treatment. I tried to put her on stronger medicine, but she didn't really see herself as needing it or didn't want to see herself as needing it. And she was afraid. People have a lot of fears about the Parkinson's medicines. Certainly if they are not administered properly, they may cause unanticipated reactions.

She was one tough patient. I tried to get her to take medicine because her symptoms were getting more pronounced: her balance was so bad and she was so slow and the tremor was there. Her husband did his best too, but she wouldn't do it. Then finally one time her husband came with her as he always did to an appointment, and we talked. He said, "She won't take anything. She needs it and it's driving me nuts." As a doctor I can't force her. And he was doing his best to convince her but was failing. While we finally convinced her to take more of her medications, it still wasn't at the level I had recommended.

There is no question about it. You need to take the medicine. As her physician, I could only make recommendations, strong ones maybe. But that didn't mean she followed them. Sometimes I tell patients, "If you are not going to follow what I tell you, then you need to find another doctor because I can't help you." There are people who are lining up to get into my practice, which is full. If patients aren't going to follow through, I tell them they need to move on.

But Lori was such a wonderful person that I never said that to her. I tried to use my powers of persuasion, but it was her husband who finally, at a moment of real crisis in their relationship, persuaded her to take the full doses of the medications we had recommended. And then she got better. She got the response from the medicine we were hoping for. And now, because of everything that she's doing and because of the tailored medication plan in place, she is actually on less medicine than she was five years ago. This is incredibly rare.

Lori

Dr. Rezak is talking about a time a few years ago when I simply wouldn't take my meds. Finally Bob and the girls read me the riot act. They let me know in no uncertain terms that Parkinson's is a family disease and that they all have it too. So I felt I had to take the meds for their sake. And I did get better when I took them. I don't like to even think about those days, so I will let Bob tell you the story.

Bob

Lori went through a very stubborn period several years ago when she refused to take her meds. Dr. Rezak had prescribed L-Dopa for her, but she wouldn't take it. Here is where her assumptions got in the way of her treatment. She thought, *If I take the meds that Rezak is recommending, they will wear off too quickly, and they won't work when I really need them.* She wanted to fight it with her own body's chemistry as long as possible. The problem was that the disease was winning, because she was increasingly exhibiting all the symptoms: tremors, falling, soft voice, all of it.

I felt helpless when she was falling all the time. I was watching her deteriorate in front of me, and there was nothing I could do about it. I would argue with her. I would argue logic with her. She is so stubborn, which is usually good news, but not in this case. It finally got to the point where I was angry all the time. Any little thing she did, I blew up. I knew it was because I was just so frustrated and scared about her not taking her meds and having to watch her slide into the abyss where neither one of us could climb out of. A negatively reinforcing cycle was setting in, and I was inept at stopping it.

Then one day, we were outside in the back, around the bird feeder, working with the flowers. She did something or said something that made me just blow up. It was just a little thing, so she said, "What are you so angry about? You are angry all the time." And I proceeded to call her every name I could imagine. I railed at her. It seemed like it went on forever. "You miserable, selfish egoist. You think you are smarter than everybody, smarter than me, smarter than the doctor, smarter than everybody else." And on and on. She had never seen me react like that. Finally it came to the threat: "You either shape up, or the nurses move in 24/7." She knew at this point that I was no longer kidding because I couldn't take it any longer. It was doing irreparable harm to her health and our relationship. We had no real relationship because she wouldn't do what I thought was her part, and she was not playing the game any longer, certainly not playing to win. So as one more example of how she's willing to change when she has to, she started taking her medication. We were back in the game, and back together.

As I look back on this terrible time when I saw my wife slipping away from us, I now realize that sometimes it's the crisis that causes the breakthrough. Even though she was just doing what she thought best, she took us to the edge of the cliff in our relationship. When we got to that perilous place, she stepped back, reexamined her assumptions, and changed. I've never been so proud of anyone in my life.

Without ever even having heard the following quote from Aeschylus that I've thought about so many times during this evolution, she proved it true, because through a crisis she has gained a special kind of insight. It expresses how sometimes we need to feel a level of pain so great that, finally, with a bit of help from above, we evolve into our higher self: "Even in our sleep, pain that cannot forget falls drop by drop upon the heart until, in our despair, and against our will, comes wisdom through the awful grace of God."

Lori

Now I am actually taking less medication than I was two years ago. Because of the systemic nature of how it all works, reducing the meds might create a new baseline, I hope. We are always juggling, always trying to keep the meds in balance. They all interact, based on my own biology. Another thing about Parkinson's meds is that they have to be taken within a very short window of time. These meds have a short half-life. If you don't take them exactly on time, you will eventually see your body's ability to function decrease. Rigidity and tremors can increase, and in the worst cases, people freeze and can't move. Luckily with me, they have a longer half-life than with many patients. I try to be very disciplined about meds. But I have more leeway than many PD patients.

I am supposed to take my meds on a carefully crafted program: before breakfast, at regularly scheduled meals, and at bedtime. Because I am largely symptom-free, I have sometimes been really very bad about taking them always at the set time, but Dr. Rezak says as long as you are not noticing a "burn off" period when the meds wear off and a "kicking in" period when they take effect, then that is okay. I know I have to get much better at taking them on schedule, so Bob has taken over organizing the medicines and reminding me to make sure to take them on time. We leave notes all over the place as reminders. Your body comes to rely on and anticipate the meds and needs to have them there at the right time.

Dr. Rezak

In Parkinson's disease, every patient is different, every patient responds to the medicines somewhat differently. We have a general idea of how people respond, but I have people who can't tolerate L-Dopa, not even half a tablet. They will just never be able to handle it. And other people who are on 2,000 milligrams quite happily. You know it is very individual. That is what I like about dealing with Parkinson's disease—each patient is unique, the way they deal with the disease is unique, and everything about it is different. But you have to take the medicine and take it in the right amount. It is hard because as Parkinson's progresses, the meds aren't always keeping up. Some days you are going to be up, some days you are going to be down. The drug might not be absorbed reliably. With Parkinson's, your GI tract might not be working as well as it should.

Also, the drugs can cause hallucinations, as they did with Lori. The drugs can make people hallucinate, but without the drugs, the patients are not going to be able to move their bodies. Then they are going to have other problems. So we used another medicine, and sometimes it counteracts the hallucinations. It is a constant balancing act. So if someone hallucinates from the L-Dopa, the question is, do you reduce it? Or do you add another drug to counteract the hallucinations, so that adds another medicine. It is very individual what we do.

Her attitude helps enormously. It is a huge part of this. She has never been the "woe is me" type. She has always been positive. She has good reason to have hope. There is new research going on, new drugs that are coming out all the time. We are not that far from a cure. We are learning more and more. In promising Parkinson's studies, the brain—say we open it and put stem cells in, stem cells that have been changed into dopamine-manufacturing cells. We could put them down into the spot where they should be. The problem is, the brain is not like the skin, where it is just melds in. Remember, every neuron has a long connection to another spot, so it is like a circuit board. How is that neuron going to make all of these long connections, especially with all the tissue in between? We don't know yet, but somebody will figure it out.

The other exciting thing on the horizon, which has already been done, is called viral vectors. These are genetic and can actually change the genetic makeup of individual cells. They take these viruses and tame them so they won't be infective. Then the researchers inject them with genetic material and insert the genetically modified viruses into specific sites in the brain. There the viruses work by getting inside the cells where they transpose that genetic piece. These viruses literally change what the cells do by inserting the new genetic material. So if you have Parkinson's disease and your cells are overactive and you get tremors, they can make them underactive. You could treat specific symptoms that way. They have now shown that these viral vectors can actually increase what they call neurotrophic factors, which is basically the fertilizer of the brain, protective growth factors. That is the stuff that protects cells so increased neurotrophic factors could ward off some of the effects of Parkinson's.

Lori

Dr. Rezak has always been positive about my case. He has always held out hope because he constantly tells me about the new research like this.

Hope is the bottom line of my contract with Parkinson's. If I buy enough time, I and thousands like me may be rewarded with a cure. Even if a cure doesn't arrive in time, I've nevertheless improved the quality of my life and the lives of those around me.

Parkinson's doesn't play fair. It has changed my life and the lives of the people I love, and that is not fair, but it is what it is. Every time I try a new medication or treatment, my foe attacks me with a different weapon. But given that I have taken on a relentless and unfair enemy, I still have hope that medical research will come to my rescue. Until it does, I will try every day to add a second, a minute, an hour, a day, a week, a month, a year, and maybe a decade of time to allow for a cure to come our way.

If you've got a terrible, unfair opponent in your life as well, don't ever waste a minute before getting into the fight to buy the time for whatever cure you need to come your way.

CHAPTER 4

Family and Friends

As AWFUL AS IT IS to have Parkinson's, Lori has never climbed this mountain alone. First and above all else of course is Bob. He and she are counterparts, together in every aspect of the struggle against Parkinson's. Lori says, "I know I would not be here if it weren't for him." When she got her diagnosis, her first thought was for Bob, fear about how this would affect him. She recognizes that there are very few good things about PD, but the best of these is the way it has pulled her family even closer. She feels blessed that Aly and Jen both live in Chicago and are such a big part of their lives and that she gets to see her grandchildren every week. That is so good for her, and she hopes for them as well.

As Dr. Lixin Sha, her acupuncturist, says, "I don't think I've ever seen a grandma like that. I'll tell you, from all the conversations we have had, because she comes every week now for fourteen years, from all she tells me, I know this is a loving family. Even though she knows how difficult this is, even though she knows there is no cure, she never puts herself in the first position. For her, from my doctor's perspective, the love they share makes the heart open and healthy."

Moreover, the Patins are blessed with a wonderful circle of friends whom they are fortunate to get to see all the time. They made many of these close friends at their church, Holy Comforter. More than half of all their friends all over the country have come from the churches in the various communities where the Patins have lived.

Lori

When I was first diagnosed, I said very little to my friends. I waited to tell them until after I had told our girls. When I did tell friends, I told the really close ones in person. I took them out to lunch and explained that PD is chronic, that probably it would proceed slowly, but eventually it would turn ugly. I let other people find out on their own. I didn't look forward to talking about it but did not want close friends to find out from someone else. Mostly I figured that the news would get around one way or another. When people do come to me to ask about PD, I am always very open and honest.

Friends have made the concept of "caring love" a reality for me. From all over the country, they contact Bob all the time to check on me. It's really sweet. Anytime something comes up, anytime we are in a bind, someone always steps up to help. They are always offering to take me places since I can't drive. They hold my arm—which is a lovely gesture, even though I don't need it anymore. They slow down when we walk. They bake and cook. The other day, someone brought a flourless chocolate cake. It was so delicious, and I haven't been able to have sweets very often because I'm allergic to wheat and gluten, so I wanted to eat the whole thing. Several times close friends have offered to stay overnight when Bob goes away. I have taken them up on it when my daughters and their children can't stay. I'm glad they just move in because I feel bad trying to rearrange other people's lives. Now my caregiver Linda moves in when Bob travels and one of the girls isn't available.

My circle of friends means so much more to me than helping hands. They enrich my and Bob's life in every way. We share our joys and sorrows and celebrate each other. If some evil giant made me choose only one spoke from the wheel that represents my fight against my hated disease, I would pick friends and family. I don't know what I would do without their love.

But let my friends speak later; first Jen, Aly, and Bob, and then my brother and sister-in-law and Bob's sister will tell more about our family because Parkinson's is truly our family's enemy.

Jen

It is a blessing we all live so close. I live fifteen to twenty minutes from Mom and Dad's house, and Aly is only thirty minutes away, unless you drive from the city at rush hour; then forget it. My four kids love it at Mom and Dad's. When Dad travels for business or for his fishing trips, the five of us move in. Mom has one of those medic alert things to wear around her neck so she can be alone during the day, but she shouldn't be sleeping without someone in the house. We five actually enjoy spending the night with her because she is who she is. This is not a burden.

Parkinson's has brought our family closer, but Mom and I were close before. My mom and I have been such good friends for so long. Still, it is definitely a blessing that Aly and I have all settled here even though this is not where we grew up.

You know, it is just one of those things that Mom is always on my mind. When I am around her, I am always aware, keeping an eye on her, making sure she's taking good care of herself. I think we inherited this kind of caring from her; it's in our "Momma-transferred DNA."

Take my dad out of the picture, and it would be a different story. To see them now is to see how lucky he actually feels to be in this battle with her, but she is extremely lucky as well to have him so "present" in this fight. He won't delegate this responsibility to others. I think one huge reason she is where she is today is because of the kind of person he is.

He is a unique combination of control freak and someone who is really scared for her safety. Dad is on her about her food, her medicine, and her exercises. He won't let her get away with anything. She pushes herself, and sometimes she does things she shouldn't, like taking care of her flowers with a watering can that is too heavy. If Dad saw that, he would get mad at her. She puts up with it from him. When situations present like this, I think, *What would Dad do?* It's kind of like the kids who wear bracelets with WWJD, meaning, What would Jesus do? Thinking about Dad helps me decide how to do the right thing for Mom.

Aly

Dad spells everything out for whomever stays with Mom when he is away. Even though it is so hard for her to accept help from anyone, this is a good example of one of those things where having her relinquish some control gives her a lot more good things in her life.

Mom and I are very close. We talk often and have our scheduled times when I always call on my way home from work, so she knows that Tuesdays and Fridays there is always going to be that phone call. Then we always try to check in at least two more times every week. My husband, Matt, and our sons, Matthew and Andrew often visit as well, including many Sundays for church and brunch afterward.

When Mom was being stubborn about not taking her meds, I told her about some of the things I see at the hospital. I see lots of people checked in because of falls. I've told her about the effects of a bad fall because one of the consequences of not taking her meds is falling. When people her age fall and break a hip or an arm so they end up in a nursing home for ten weeks, they are in real trouble, and sometimes it's the beginning of the end of their independence. But she continued to hold out and not take her meds. And fall.

Finally Dad had a plan. He called a family meeting where he announced, "We are approaching this disease from now on as a family. It is a disease that affects every one of us in unique ways, and Lori, you can't be in control of it yourself." From that time on, we started making more decisions as a family. I think this was a turning point. In this reality, we acknowledge that we all have Parkinson's and must deal with it together in ways that are supportive of everyone in the entire family. In a very real sense, we rise or fall together.

Bob

The girls are fabulous. I think this struggle has drawn all of us around Lori, but even more around each other. I rely on the girls more now than I ever used to. They are strong, intelligent and resourceful women. I ask for their advice and their counsel, and I listen more. We are together, and we approach each other on an adult-to-adult level with each other, no longer parents standing above children. Out of necessity has come a blessing. This takes work and effort, but the payoff is that we are closer than we have ever been. We are dealing better with this challenge together as a family. And any challenge to come. We'll be there because there's still no cure for Parkinson's.

Now, what Lori and I have is what I'll describe as a "primal" relationship. By this I mean that, at its core, this is about not only individual but also joint survival. We both have to survive this. Because this is all-out war, our relationship has to be an almost overwhelming relationship in the sense that we have to be absolutely bonded in both our common life and in this struggle. Most fortunately, there was a firm foundation to our relationship before this disease and will be one beyond it as well.

Still, we are so vastly different. Lori describes our relationship as two gigantic cogs whose gears must mesh even though they have significant differences in size and shape. The only way to make the cogs work is to knock the edges off so our set of skills and behaviors become complementary. For example, I am much more open with my emotions while she is more private. I think we are both really tough yet vulnerable, but in different ways. She will suffer in silence, whereas I want to get aggressive. She is heavily grounded in an internal, close-in world with a strong focus on "now" and "us." While I respect and love that, I am grounded in the external world and in the longer term. For another example, we solve problems differently. While Lori's approach is more intuitive, I bring process to our battle with Parkinson's because I learned it of necessity in the business world. I will tell you more about the process of our mutual attack on Parkinson's in the next chapter.

Because we are bringing every resource we have into the fight against the disease, we have to work together. In effect, we are now like two horses in tandem pulling the same wagon. If we try to deal with the "big ugly" separately, the wagon won't move forward, and we'll just pull each other apart. I think one of our most difficult challenges is understanding that each of us is now in harness with somebody else and nothing either of us does will work unless we pull together. That sounds great until you factor in that Lori is so independent that it bothers her enormously to depend on anybody, particularly me.

Given my natural tendency to be a control freak, Lori and I have learned that I am going to do things she doesn't like, such as yelling "stop" when she is carrying things with both hands while walking down the stairs. She needs one hand free to grab the railing in case she starts to fall. She knows, I hope, that I am not intending to be bossy. When I say, "What are you doing?" it is not intended to mean, "I am your master." It is intended to be about her safety. Unless there is a constant series of reminders about everyday safety, she will just forget because she thinks she is fine. She has learned to tolerate my bossiness, which has been a big challenge for her. Now she will let it go because she knows, at the very least, that I mean well.

So when I say that Parkinson's has been the teacher, here is the kind of lesson I am thinking about. It starts with a philosophy taught to me by those much wiser that there is very little in life you can't turn to your advantage if you think about it the right way. You learn that there are things over which you have no control, so you simply have to adjust to these. There are things you can control if you do it the right way. Finally, there are things that you will never control if you present them in the wrong way.

Lori tells me when I am getting it wrong so I can recognize the difference. I have learned—maybe—to present things in a fashion that is tolerable to her. And she has learned to accept that she must make constant adjustments as well or we'll be fighting the current battle with out-of-date weapons.

Let me give you an example of my own "learning up." I have developed amazing peripheral vision. I can stare straight ahead yet know exactly where she is and what she is doing, and I can grab her in an instant if it looks like she'll fall. This is a new talent. I could never have done this before.

It is not all about my being a watchdog who deals with Lori's disease simply as a series of problems to be solved. Because of Parkinson's, we have also developed certain habits together that have brought unexpected joy. Every morning I get up early to make her a hearty breakfast. By hearty, I mean steak or eggs or lamb chops or hot cereal because she needs to eat a lot of protein. Keeping her weight up is a constant challenge. We weigh her every morning and plan the day's meals accordingly. Then I bring breakfast up to her on a tray to eat in bed or while doing her first set of exercises. After she is finished, I help her shower. She's especially cute naked. Then I wash and blow-dry her hair. I even scrunch it and use a diffuser. (Even though years ago I would have had no idea what those terms meant!) I have really gotten good at it. The girls say Lori goes to Chez Robert (pronounced Shay Ro-BEAR). If anybody would have told me that one of the highlights of my day would be being a hair stylist, I would have said, "You've got to be nuts. And whatever you do, please don't tell the guys!" Yet it has become an incredibly intimate moment, one that we have both come to cherish.

I was thinking the other morning as I was doing Lori's hair that here is the opportunity to make the point to other men that, unlike whatever they might be thinking, hair dressing might be very fulfilling to their masculine ego. Trust me on this, guys. To put it bluntly, doing their wife's hair might prove a big boon to their sex life. My counsel to them, man to man, would be to adopt the practice in their own selfish best interest. There is no better prelude to "intimacy" than being with a beautiful woman as she steps out of the shower with little to nothing on. As the warm air flows over her head and you work your fingers through her hair, etc., you have a good chance of being able to promote a "flow" toward other possible intimate events. While Lori might be a bit embarrassed by such disclosure, I don't have any reservations about admitting that a "real man" must take advantage of any and all opportunities. I'm even thinking that there might even be a franchise opportunity here, "Hair (and more) by Real Men." Look, guys, if you want to have a testosterone festival, you've got to get creative!

And then there are nights where both of us get very little sleep because of the sleep disturbances called "REM sleep disorder," which is part of Parkinson's. When people have this symptom, it's not passive—they actually act out their dreams. To them, their dreams are real. In Lori's case, sometimes she talks a lot; others she acts out her dreams. Unfortunately, she never says, "Kiss me again, Bob," or "Let's have another child." There are nights when she is perfectly fine and sleeps like a rock, but then there are times when she can be chatty and other nights where she gets physical with me. Once I woke her up because she was choking me with the cord from my sleep apnea device. When I asked her why, she said, "You're the dog. I am taking you for a walk." Another time she awakened me with her hand, pulling up and down on my arm. This time she told me I was a chicken leg and she was skinning me. Funny to be sure, but not so funny at 2:00 a.m.

If she is going to be really, really busy in her sleep, sometimes I just lie there and have two or three business conversations in my head. I problem-solve. I think, *Okay, I've got this project. Who is governing this thing? What are the board's negotiation terms? How am I going to manage this executive coaching process?* Other times I goof off and semi-dream about things that cannot be described in a family book. If I have been up a long time in the night, in the middle of the day I will crash on the couch for half an hour.

REM sleep disorder is part of the whole picture—you can be angry about this stuff or you can change yourself and accept it.

It is your choice. You can let it bother you or you can accept that it is simply Parkinson's. Anyone thrown into this type of problem needs to become a "challenge-adjusted" learner. This means you reexamine your assumptions and honestly assess reality and remake the plan for each new set of circumstances. If you hold to the old plan to confront new challenges, you'll just compound the emerging problem.

Then, among the blessings of our situation, there is her relationship with others, where she gives and receives love and affection and attention and encouragement. There's the family and the church and the connection to friends, people who are very proud of her, people who watch out for her. A few years ago, when she was not doing all that well, we would pull up in front of church before she would go in for the shawl ministry. Her friends would be looking out the window, waiting for her so somebody could go out and walk her in. That is just what they do. So Lori has this set of friends who tell her she may have a disability, but that's okay and they love her anyway. It doesn't matter that she has PD; in fact, they may actually love her more because she hasn't let the disease distract her from loving them back.

Someone wise once told me she'd like to live her life so that she put in more than she took out. Lori has put so much more into my life than I'll ever be able to pay back. But it's worth a shot . . . and thanks to what she's doing to stave off Parkinson's, I still have time.

And of course of all our friends, perhaps our former rector at Holy Comforter, Bob Myers, knows us best in certain ways, certainly spiritually and on a level most people don't. We'll hear from him at the end of this chapter. First let's check in with Lori's younger brother, his wife, and my sister, and then several close friends.

Don and Jeanette Cedik

Don: I think you would expect to see a lot of changes in a Parkinson's patient, but I think my sister is quite remarkable in that she didn't let PD change her life at all. She didn't let it slow her down. But Lori is a person who cannot sit still. She has to be doing something all the time. She was always like that. She's a real fighter, or she would have given up a long time ago. Her husband is right there by her side 24/7, and he is a remarkable guy too.

Last summer we were really, really concerned. I went to visit many nights when she was in the hospital. Even as miserable as she must have felt, she never showed it, but that is Lori. At one really low point, I think she was able to recognize people, but she didn't show much of a reaction when she saw them. She is so much better now. Even the doctors are amazed. Where she is and where she should be are miles apart.

Let me tell you about how amazing Lori was when our mom was sick. When Mom lived in Florida and Lori lived in Chicago, she used to call her mother twice a day to help her take her medication because she had grown forgetful. Lori would call her and say, "Take your pills." So Mom would take the pills while she was on the phone with Lori. Lori was diagnosed with Parkinson's while Mother was still alive, but Lori never told her. Since Mom was suffering from her own ailments, Lori felt she didn't need any more worries.

I think the biggest lesson that I have learned from this whole escapade is, if life throws you a curve ball, you don't have to strike out. Stand up there and deal with it. It may be short term or it might be a major bump in the road but learn to deal with it. You have a choice: deal with it or not. I have learned from my sister that fighting is way better than giving in. Lori is a lot stronger than I could ever be. When bad things come up, you don't run and hide from them. You do what you can because life goes on. You have got to make the best of what you have. Lori has done that so well that it is scary. If she can pass that drive on to other people, that would be great.

Even though she seems almost nonchalant about her Parkinson's, I am sure she is not. Still, somebody who doesn't know her probably wouldn't know that she has it. If I had PD, I would be in the corner with my thumb in my mouth, crying.

I think my sister is an inspiration.

Jeanette: I was suspicious something was wrong even before Lori told us she had PD. We had been up there visiting them a few months before they told us. I didn't say anything to Don at the time, but in my mind I just had a feeling that something wasn't right. She had started to tremble noticeably. I never mentioned it because I didn't want to worry anybody. Then that Christmas, they called and told us. They had been to the doctor several times and found out what the problem was. If she ever did break down or anything, it was never, ever in front of anyone.

Don: No, it was just as if she was telling us she had a hangnail.

Jeanette: Lori is so proud. I told her, "It's not that we are trying to take away your self-sufficiency and pride when we do something for you. We're trying to make it easier for you so everybody is happy and you stay safe."

Before Lori had Parkinson's, she was always very health conscious. I think because she was so active, she was also always perhaps too thin. Also she had problems with her stomach for a long time that made it difficult for her to eat much. It took her a long time to figure out that she needs to be on a gluten-free diet that she has adopted, again showing us her willingness to adapt. As a result of the gluten-free diet, she can eat more and I think she looks the best that she has ever looked in the whole time I have known her—which is forty years.

Polly Patin-Mellor

Lori has always stood beside Rob—I call my brother Rob even though everyone else calls him Bob—and he says he would be nothing without her. I think he does that as a habit—giving other people the credit.

Lori is like Rob in that she has to be busy all the time. Sometimes, however, because she believes she is just fine, she can be reckless. For instance, going up the stairs carrying heavy things without any help is a reckless act for Lori. One time when I was visiting, Lori was carrying a full load of laundry up stairs and slipped. She would have fallen if I hadn't been on the steps.

Having Parkinson's has been very hard on her because she wants to do everything herself; she hates being dependent on people. She doesn't like the restrictions that everybody puts on her because of Parkinson's. She is a very capable person and likes to be in charge of her own life. Now she doesn't have control over many aspects of her life anymore and needs to have somebody with her most of the time.

Parkinson's has changed both of them. Rob has become even more attentive to her. He won't let her do anything that is in any way dangerous. Lori does everything possible to combat that disease. She keeps herself very active and disciplined.

The worst time was when Lori was in a coma. Then they had to put her in a nursing home. I thought she was not going to survive, but she did. Not only did she survive, she thrived. When she was there, she even took care of the other patients. When she came out of the coma, she had to be fed three meals a day. Before that, Lori had never eaten that much. The fact that she has gained the weight has improved her overall health, clearly helping with the Parkinson's.

Before Lori had Parkinson's, she was very independent, and so was Rob. He was out doing his things, and she was out doing hers. They passed each other in the night, so to speak. Now Rob is her caretaker. Lori, I know, has a problem when people try to take too much control of her, such as people telling her that she has to pick up her feet when she walks. So she has had to learn to rely on others. She has handled that well also, even though you can see she gets frustrated sometimes. I think she's so focused on the Parkinson's disease and handling it that she kind of forgets about everything else.

Rob and Lori have a very strong marriage. It hasn't come easy at times. It has been hard work, but they sure do love one another.

I admire her greatly.

Chuck and Jeanne Johnson

Chuck: We are so glad Lori is telling the story of how she fights Parkinson's, and we are honored to be part of this because the story is so special.

We first met the Patins at church when we started going to Holy Comforter in 1997. Lori must have been just recently diagnosed. She was shaking a little back then. The tremors came and went. We saw them at services and then at the coffee hour afterward. After we saw them in a couples group, we started sitting with them during services. On the way to communion, Bob would lead the way, always looking over his shoulder to make sure she was okay. Years ago, it was not all that easy for her to climb the steps as you get to the altar. While he actually escorted her, he would let her struggle up the steps on her own, looking over his shoulder to make sure she was okay.

Soon we started socializing with them on a much deeper level. We would share stories about our lives and our children, the good and the bad, so we have really gotten to know them. But in doing that, we've seen Lori with the ups and downs with the disease over many years.

Lori loves to throw parties for friends. When she invites people over, she is always inclusive, never exclusive. They're both that way, probably more than any people I have ever known. And so much fun.

Jeanne: When I think of Lori, I think pride, but the good kind. When maybe she was having a little trouble doing something, you would want to help make it easier, but she would politely let you know, "Don't help; I will take care of it." But the way in which she would let you know, however, it was just fine. Let me give an example.

Once the four of us went to a dance in the city. Because it was in the city, Lori carried her dance shoes. When she was trying to buckle her shoes in the ladies' room, one side was easier than the other. Since it was taking her a while, I made the mistake of asking her if she would like me to do that shoe. She looked up at me, smiled, and said, "I'm getting it." And I realized, oh no, she would never say, "Don't do that." I would have let the person know, "Thank you very much, I'm doing it myself." But she didn't, so I didn't chastise myself and think, *Why did I do that?* She did it with such grace that she never made me feel bad.

Chuck: I have a great image of Bob. When they came to visit us here, we took them into New York to see *La Cage*, a Broadway musical, during a hard rain. The only place I could pull over anywhere near the curb was beside a huge puddle. Bob had to spirit her out of the car to get her past that. He had to stand in the puddle, but nonetheless he picked her up, swooping her out of the car and over the puddle, and carried her into the theater.

Jeanne: They are quite a team, just a miraculous couple. They have done a ton of research on PD, and Lori is trying to do something every day to work on this, to battle PD—exercising, playing the harp, not to mention dancing. At the same time she enjoys life. Whenever we see her, she lights up. You know, she is just a joyful, loving, determined, happy person in spite of this.

Anne and Tom Heynen

Anne: From the beginning Lori was open about her Parkinson's, yet she has never appeared to want sympathy. She always has a smile on her face. I am not just saying this because it's going into a book. I'm not trying to sugarcoat it. She doesn't complain about anything.

We first met Bob and Lori at Holy Comforter Church before she was even diagnosed with Parkinson's. Our friendship developed slowly over time. I feel very much that they really genuinely like us as people, and I feel that Lori likes me very much. That makes me feel good because she is very loyal. I am quite a bit older than Lori. I am kind of like her older sister.

Tom: Bob fills in all the little pieces for Lori. That man has totally dedicated his life to her. Let me give you an example. When the four of us were playing golf recently, he would come over and help her by putting her ball on the tee—a small thing, but so necessary for Lori, and a good indication of how attuned he is to her abilities.

Linda Hilton

I am Lori's caregiver. I help out by driving Lori and by staying with her when Bob is out of town. I met them when Lori was in the Mather Home in rehab because my mother was staying there too. I just immediately liked her when she popped in to my mother's room to visit, so I would take Mom to visit her and Bob too. Now I feel like their third daughter.

Lori never gets angry, ever. She is also a great person to confide in. I could tell her anything and she would not tell a soul. And if you try to get dirt about other people from her, forget it.

She and Bob are both honest, really caring. They would do anything for you. Like one day she knew I was really upset about something. She got me a card and wrote a nice message. Since she mailed it, I didn't get it for two days, but when it arrived it meant a lot that she could be that caring of her own caregiver.

Tom and Judy Hamilton

Judy: Lori doesn't like people even mentioning PD. When all of us women are together, we look out for her. It's just something we do. Without even thinking about it, we just get up to go to the ladies' room with her if Bob can't. She doesn't like you to hold on to her because she wants to do it herself.

She doesn't feel entitled one bit because she has Parkinson's. Let me give an example. Once at a church party at her house, she fell and I was holding her. We actually called the paramedics because she had a serious gash. If it happened to any of us, most of us without Parkinson's would have said, "You know what, you guys, go on with the party. I am going to the ER." Not Lori. She wouldn't go with the paramedics. She told them, "I need this party more than going with you." Then she just moved over to the screened porch and put her feet up on a bag of ice. The party went on. She is not at all hesitant to tell you what she needs. It helps; it helps a ton.

Tom: Judy and I are appreciative of who they are and how precious this relationship is. Very seldom do you sit down and review fifteen years of a relationship. When we did, we were reminded of how instrumental and how precious it really is. A friendship like ours is a once-in-a-lifetime kind of thing. It is the kind of reason you don't ever move from where you live.

They are just very special people. We are fortunate to be friends with them. It's a marvelous and blessed friendship.

Getting to know them was a slow thing. They don't overwhelm you. They let you come to them, and then they come to you in a slow process. Bob has always been open and generous, so you know him right away. Once you do, they are a lot of fun. Bob played a lot of jokes.

We got him back. I am the guy who put the full bath in the back of Bob's truck. Bob Myers got involved too. We put bales of hay and beer cans and girly magazines all over the truck while he was in church. Lori passed the keys to me at communion in church so that I could get the truck open to do what I needed to do. To get us back, Bob had signs made for his truck. First, he drove around with a sign saying, "Northshore Plumbing and Proctology. Dr. Robert K. Myers and Dr. Thomas Hamilton. We'll fix your pipes. Call 1-800 BIG OUCH." Then he plastered his truck with "Kenilworth Taxidermy and Veterinary. Dr. Robert Myers and Dr. Thomas Hamilton. Give us your pets; either way you get them back. Call 1-800 PET BACK."

With all the things the Patins could do and all the places they could go and all the things they have, they never lose their focus on the genuineness of their relationship. For the Patins, this is the very basis. They are well rounded. They don't fool around; no frills. They don't let anything distract them from what they want to accomplish in their lives.

Judy: Lori's Parkinson's doesn't stop them from living. Even though it is obviously part of their lives, they don't let it be an overwhelming part. They just deal with it. And I think one of the big reasons they can do this is there is so much love and support from that whole family.

Tom: We have been friends with them for fifteen years, about the same amount of time as Lori has had her diagnosis. In all that time, Bob and Lori never shut down socially or in their communication. They never changed the way they related to us, or from what we could tell, the way they related to their family or future. They never modified it at all. It was set sometime earlier in their lives.

Normally when you are struck with a life-changing condition like this, you back up a little and shut down a little and gather your resources.

Before I turn the podium over to Rector Bob Myers, let me tell you about one of the crucial chapters in our relationship with the Patins. Maybe three years ago, Bob Myers's wife, Bonnie, passed away after a long battle with several bouts of a unique form of brain cancer. The two couples—Bob and Lori, and Judi and me—kind of became the caring spectators. We did everything we possibly could to help comfort the Myerses. And it was especially touching that Aly, the Patins' nurse/daughter, was the last person Bonnie saw before each of her brain operations and the first person she saw when she woke up.

We weren't there when Bonnie died, but when it was close, Bob Myers called Bob and Lori, Judy and me, and two other couples and asked us to come over as he performed the last rites. We were grateful to be able to tell Bonnie we loved her. She died later that evening. I think sharing an event in life like that joins us in a profound way.

Bob Myers

I first met the Patins when they joined Holy Comforter. It must have been about twenty years or so ago because their house was under construction. I found them very delightful. My first impression was that they are a very easy couple to connect with. They obviously are people with some means, but they were informal, welcoming. We just pulled chairs up around boxes because the house wasn't finished. I had a very strong, immediate, warm, friendly, inviting response.

Since then I have worked with Bob very closely because he has been involved in the development of the parish. I have also worked with Lori in some of the educational pieces and with a fund-raiser, the rummage sale. She was active in the church's adult education program and with the flower guild. She is an amazing flower arranger. I love both of them very much. My wife, Bonnie, who died three years ago, was very fond of the Patin family too. Bonnie was the director of the school of nursing at Evanston Hospital, where their daughter is now a nurse.

They are two of the funniest practical jokers. Early on, humor became a big part of our relationship. What was most delightful is when we stopped exchanging real gifts and decided to give gag gifts instead. None of us needed anything else. If we did, we would prefer to go and buy what we wanted. They have given us some of the most amazing, creative, and sometimes disgusting gifts.

They are so generous. They open their home on a regular basis to a myriad of activities for family and friends. They put on a New Year's Eve party and invite all their friends. They open their home twice each year for church activities, including our parish's big summer beach party. The event takes over their whole backyard and beach, including Bob's boat out on the lake. He drives the boat, and not always well. He nearly lost his thumb one year docking, not to mention his bad fall running down the stairs to the beach the summer before last. He means well despite his tendency to run into things.

They are not just financially generous and generous with their things and their home, but you could ask them for anything and they would be there in a minute. Not just for a select few but for everybody. Bob coaches young, professional people in the parish on a regular basis. They call on him for counsel as sometimes they are seeking new jobs or are in fear of losing their jobs, and sometimes they are under great stress. He led the men's fraternity, which was a group of forty or so men who came every Friday morning from six to seven thirty for a program about what it means to be a man in the world today, and how to be committed to your family, your work, yourself, and your faith.

In my experience, Bob is as passionate about this struggle against Parkinson's as Lori is. I think PD would have been fatal for Lori if Bob were not in the picture.

Although Lori is reluctant to tell it, her story has universal appeal. She says, "My story is no different than anybody else's. Lots of people face Parkinson's or worse; and a lot of people do it courageously."

I reply, "Yes, that is true. I just may not know other people with Parkinson's, but you for some reason have been blessed to face it the way you do, and you are especially blessed to have the resources to tell your story."

I think the strongest message about Lori and Bob's story is a love story between a man and a woman who face life's adversities with open eyes. They never lose sight of the big things, the things that are truly important even though this has not been the only issue in their life. They have dealt with many things, so it is not as though they have had a life free of bruises and bumps, hurts and pains. Suddenly this happened, and this was their response in the context of a much bigger life journey. It is a story of love between two people who passionately care about one another and who refuse to give in. And it is a love that is not defined by their faith. It is bigger than that.

My experience with Bob and Lori Patin is one of two people who are deeply and passionately in love and willing to sacrifice for each other. The character of love at its deepest and broadest level is sacrificial. If someone has the capacity for sacrifice, it means, "I do something that will cost me even though I won't get paid back." So I would say the purpose, as I see it, in telling their story is to show that is what these two people do for each other: they give so the other can thrive.

There is a whole array of other things that describe these two. Courage is one. When they received the diagnosis and struggled to understand it, they searched with the tenacious, steadfast capacity to pursue every avenue; for example, they go to great lengths to find the right doctor. I wondered why on earth these two drive more than an hour away to Central DuPage Hospital. The reason is, in their own words, "We will go wherever we need to go to find the best person we can and look at the results, whatever they may be." So it is the kind of courage that is tenacious and steadfast.

I think another part of their story is honesty. They have been honest with all of us. It wasn't just with me and with their family; they were honest with everybody. They tell their friends, "This is what we are struggling with." They are this open and honest, not in a sense of inappropriate disclosure, but appropriately. They are not sensationalizing their story; rather, they are honestly recording it in a way that really invited us all on their journey. The second part of their honesty is that you cannot experience a disease like this, particularly in its darker moments, without frustration and irritation. Anger—they were honest about that too. And they are open with each other about their anger. It takes a lot of courage to be able to be honest and forthright, particularly with so-called negative feelings. This gives them emotional strength because they deal with the issues emotionally, allowing themselves to be down when they need to be down, allowing themselves to be irritated with each other the way they need to be. He pushes her to do more; she pushes back, saying "get off my back." That kind of honesty.

And then they are spiritually strong, in the sense of living with a perspective that life doesn't have any guarantees, so that each says, "I am going to give it all I have and hope for the best. If this is what life gives me, then I'm truly a blessed person." That's the story Lori wants to tell.

Lori and Bob have deep faith, and that faith is principally faith in each other. Each knows the other can be trusted. They're loyal to each other. They're dedicated to each other. They're compassionate about each other. I think these are two people who embody the faith they have in each other. They have deep commitment, trust, and faith in the human family, starting certainly with their own family and then their extended family and their church. They expect that people will look to the good.

Bob always says, and Lori, in her own way, says the same thing, "If there is a problem, let's always and perpetually look for the solution." That is how they approach life, and that is how they have approached this disease.

Love, courage, honesty, spiritual strength, faith—this is their story. It happens to play out in the Parkinson's, but it plays out that way as a mirror of the people they are. All these virtues were playing out in their lives long before Parkinson's and will play out through Parkinson's and beyond.

CHAPTER 5

---⬦⬦⬦---

Caregivers

THIS CHAPTER IS ANOTHER FORM of a classic love story.

A devoted cadre of caregivers marches beside Lori uphill against Parkinson's. Between friends and family and caregivers, there is also a lot of stepping into each others' shoes. Her caregivers have become her friends over the years, and members of her family have become her caregivers.

Above and beyond medical treatment, Lori has explored many alternative therapies. Some she rejected because they didn't seem to help. Currently Lori sticks with three professional caregivers who treat her every week. She goes to Debbie Campbell for deep-tissue massage; Cheryl Becker for Feldenkrais®[2] (a somatic educational approach to human movement, learning, and change) lessons; and Dr. Lixin Sha for acupuncture. Debbie was helpful in getting her started with several of her caregivers, such as Dr. Sha, as well as with a nutritionist, a homeopath, and an herbalist. She has also worked with a physical therapist, although not at present as now she is so much better. She takes harp lessons to improve control of her fingers, lifts weights to develop strength, and studies tai chi and takes ballroom dancing lessons to work on balance. And of course Lori also has Linda, who cares for Lori by driving her, staying with her when Bob is away, and by generally looking out for her welfare.

---

[2]   Feldenkrais Method® and Guild Certified Feldenkrais Practitioner are registered trademarks of the Feldenkrais® Guild.

Not only does participating in these therapies take a lot of time, it also costs a lot of money. Lori wants to make it clear that her message is not to go get every therapist. She knows she is very lucky that her family has the financial resources to explore all these therapies, but it is the exploration in and of itself that makes a difference—that and the dedication to fighting the disease. Planning an attack and then attacking the disease in a logical, determined fashion is a form of therapy itself.

Is there any proof that these therapies are helping reverse the disease and keeping her Parkinson's under control? To some degree, yes. When Lori goes to the neurologist for a four-month checkup and gets an A plus, it is absolute proof that some things beyond the medications are helping. Can she prove that one therapy is the magic potion? No. But at the same time, she doesn't have proof that they are not helping, both individually and collectively. As long as she is feeling good, she is going to continue with them in good faith. If all these treatments and lessons help Lori maintain a few degrees above where she was before, they are worth all the effort.

Lori

As I try to honor people who have truly saved me from a life of gradual deterioration into the abyss of Parkinson's, I must devote words to thank, celebrate, and sit at the feet of those who care for me.

As for my caregivers, let's start with Bob. There's an old gospel song that goes, "He walks with me and he talks with me and he tells me I am his own." The song is about a much greater force than any person, but I love the language as it also feels a lot like someone I know here at home.

Bob

If anyone would have told me years ago that "caregiver" would be the most challenging job I'd ever have, I'd have laughed. Compared to the challenges of business? Impossible. The stress couldn't be remotely as bad. The rush of adrenaline that comes from crisis management would surely be missing. Certainly competing with other tough players in the marketplace would trump any role of just taking care of somebody. That's what I thought, but I was wrong about all of it.

Let me just admit this: I've faced a lot of really big challenges over a business career with a lot of responsibility and money and people's lives at stake, but being a caregiver is the toughest thing I have ever done—by far. It's tougher intellectually because I'm an amateur at it, and there is so much to learn and so many variables, and I haven't been trained to do them. Past experience is no help.

Also, the level of stress is compounded because it's personal and critical. This is not about some balance sheet or a return on some shareholder's investment—no matter how important, these balances and returns are abstractions after all. Caregiving means literally the life and death of the woman I love. There are emotions at work that drain my energy, keep me up at night, and test me every day. It is also so sad because there is this sense of loss: what it takes away, the options it removes from both of you. I've never once cried over a business situation, but I've cried over Parkinson's.

What has helped me a lot as a caregiver is a core business concept that some very smart people taught me: it isn't the strongest or the most intelligent who survive and prosper but those with the ability to adapt and change.

Still, I have an almost bipolar reaction to being a caregiver. It is the best of jobs and the worst of jobs. It tears you up in some very tough ways, but it can put you back together as a better person than you could ever have imagined.

In all candor, I admit I have struggled to adjust to the role. It has tested me emotionally at a level hard to describe. It has forced me to change in ways I did not anticipate; I have made changes that I hope are for the better. Thanks to blessings only gradually understood at the time but now deeply valued, I am lucky I did not just deflect the caregiver job to others until either emotional or financial resources ran out.

To begin with, I'm a guy. We are not necessarily programmed by Mother Nature to do this stuff easily. We're hunters more than nurturers. We lack patience. Many of us are control freaks. And I was all of that. It took Lori years to get me trained not to embarrass her in public.

By the time Lori clearly had Parkinson's, I was in my fifties. I felt good about the person I had become and didn't have much interest in changing who I was or how I operated. My life at home was based on the assumption that I'd spend my formative years in the business marketplace while Lori would win in her world. Then we'd ride off into the sunset essentially different but healthy and happy and without much need to alter who we would be. It was a shock to realize it wasn't going to work out that way. The most difficult part of it has been to deal with the lack of control over our destiny. We have had to face disillusionment, particularly giving up the selfish assumption that, as we got older, we would largely live a life of rather significant influence, if not dominance, over our last chapter. Looking back, that assumption was really naïve.

I think one of the hardest things about being a caregiver is to hate the disease, really loathe it, but not to resent the person who has it. You may know intellectually that it is not his or her fault, but every caregiver has moments of thinking, *Why me? What did I do to deserve this?* So, being realistic and human, periodically you will take a walk in the wallow. It's inevitable. Then you gotta set that aside and move on, for yourself as much as the person you are caring for. To underestimate the challenge of dealing with your emotions would be not only naïve but potentially destructive.

Another huge issue for me has been to learn the art of patience. Let me give you some background here. As a young Catholic lad, I was told that being late for Mass was a mortal sin and you'd go to hell for that and being late for anything else was a venial sin and those added up to be mortal sins and you'd go to hell for those too. As a result, I've left lines at the movie theater if they're too long. I've left Lori at home once or twice when she wasn't ready when she said she would be and later paid the appropriate price for it. But since she has been diagnosed, I have realized that Lori can feel my impatience and then she'll move too quickly, creating the risk of a fall. This has taught me that I had better figure out other ways to occupy my mind while I wait for her. Solving business problems in my head works. I also take deep breaths and calm myself with soothing thoughts of the glass of wine waiting at the end of that eventual drive. She does her part by trying to be on time as she knows being late still drives me nuts. I reciprocate by not doing the things that drive her bonkers like blurting out the "Hey, we're about to be late again" mistake. We have learned that there is a special rhythm to the dance of patience.

With my background and experience, I also have a tendency to bring a business process to any problem, and that is what I've fallen back on with Parkinson's. First, do your research. Start trying to figure out what this challenge means. Then devise a plan to take action to meet the challenge. What is so devastating about this disease, however, is that it is progressive and incurable. So it's much different than a "line of sight" problem with a short-term game plan with an expected end and a clear way to measure success. Here, we are in for a long and complicated fight. The prognosis sets the stage for the challenge. It doesn't kill you quickly, but it makes your life miserable. So we must keep adjusting as the disease progresses, trying to figure out how we strategically position ourselves so that Lori gets the best possible care at each stage of the disease's evolution. Next, Lori and I have taken stock of what we have in terms of resources. We are unbelievably lucky, first of all, because we have Lori. She is the fundamental resource in dealing with this. With her attitude and determination, we actually have a reasonable chance to win this fight. In addition, we are blessed to have the resources to be able to attack it on many fronts and have made the decision that we will do whatever it takes to fight this hateful disease. If we have to compromise elsewhere, so be it. We can use proven and reliable therapies, and we also have discovered other therapies beyond conventional Western medicine. We keep searching—it is what you do with an evolving enemy.

I was trained long ago in the world of work that you can use any situation to your advantage if you approach it the right way. In this case, with Parkinson's, we say to ourselves, "We acknowledge that this is ugly, but how do we actually make it work for us?" How do we force ourselves to get into a mindset that says that we can turn this ugly situation to our advantage by thinking about it creatively? We asked, "How do we use this to strengthen our relationship? How do we find ways to support research that may pay off soon enough? How can we find a way to deal with several symptoms with a single therapy?"

So we confront Parkinson's as we would any major challenge. There has to be a strategy. There has to be an action plan. It has to make sense. There have to be compromises. Because it's an iterative challenge—meaning the challenge will keep repeating—we'll perpetually need to adjust. Get used to it; make it a habit.

Other than hairstyling (ha, ha), I have learned an immense amount from being a caregiver, and it has certainly made me a better man. Now I'm even somewhat embarrassed to admit that I used to think that the business battles were the truly big ones in life. Not to diminish them, but that was before I discovered Parkinson's. This thing has challenged me at my core and increased my humility in ways I could not have possibly imagined.

I've also learned that I have to do everything I can to take away Lori's worries because Lori is an Olympic medal–winning worrier. Also I'm learning to do it without telling her too often, "Don't worry; I've got it taken care of." She will worry anyway because that's in her nature, and that's not good if you have Parkinson's. Anxiety eats her energy; then she gets tired; and then she falls. I'm still learning to try to anticipate what might make her anxious and solve the issue if I can in advance or assure her that there will be a plan to deal with her concerns when we need one.

I have also had to learn to adjust the rhythm of my life to hers. I have learned to get up early and set things in motion so I can be more effective later as to how we deal with our day. When she wakes up, it's breakfast, it's the shower, it's the hair, it's the weighing, it's the making sure today's events are all covered. We've learned that we have to be careful about schedules so that we both know everything that is going on. And it requires more than a little flexibility to accommodate everything and everybody. If I am committed to spending time with a client and all of a sudden discover something that needs to be done for Lori that she didn't tell me, that is stressful for me, and as a result, for her too. So we have to work very hard to make sure we have communicated everything we need to do and that we don't make commitments we can't handle. Communication has had to become an art form, but the side benefit is that now we're better at it perhaps than we ever have been in almost fifty years of marriage. I've even learned that when I say something and she says "What?" it's not because she didn't hear me. She said it because she's giving me a chance to change what I said!

I believe and hope Lori and I are closer than we have ever been. It's a matter of giving some things up to get where we need to be. We understand what the larger goal is. In my case, I have had to redefine success. Although I have been trained in the business terms of success, now success is no longer win/lose. Now, even though I might need to be working on a consulting project, I say, "Let's go to the movies," because the definition of time changes when you don't know how much time you have left. Everything becomes fast-forward. You learn to adapt to the reality that you may not have all that much time left. Balancing all you need to do within this new concept of time requires flexibility and flow and an adjustment process that have taught me things that have actually made me a better consultant. It is a precious gift that I could not have anticipated.

During the early years after Lori was diagnosed, I still needed to work. In my last assignment I cut a three-year deal with my company because I knew I couldn't commit myself any longer than that at the level the job demanded when Lori would need me the way she would at the rate the disease was progressing. I left the company with their blessing in 2004. It had become clear that I needed more time to focus on Lori since I wanted to be her primary caregiver. I'll admit I had no real idea of what that would entail.

Before I retired, I incorporated my little one-man-band consulting company, The Bottom Line Club (TBLC), because I wanted to have a corporate structure in place that would allow me to do any one of a number of business ventures on a part-time basis. I slowly developed a consulting practice because I knew intuitively that I would still need the intellectual stimulation of some kind of work as well as the feeling that I still make a difference in the world. TBLC lets me do it within the boundaries of my commitment to Lori. We have both realized that I have to have my own "thing" to some degree or I'll dry up intellectually and grow to resent the situation at home.

I also have come to realize that I have to have a certain amount of time to myself beyond work, so I take a few fishing trips mostly with semi-insane people who are a great distraction from the challenges at home. I have found that if I do these things for myself, I return energized to the challenge and reward of caregiving.

If I didn't allow myself certain extracurricular activities, I would then be forced to systematically give up things that still provide joy, hope, stimulation, and the ego satisfaction of feeling like I am still relevant in the world beyond home. On the one hand, I hope I have moved from being relevant in one sphere to trying to be relevant in another. But to have totally given up the first sphere without some replacement of intellectual stimulation and people connections would have been, in the end, destructive to the cause of caring for my lady. That is one of the reasons I have needed Linda, Lori's caretaker. Her value is that she buys me time, which gives me room in my schedule to do my things and stay essentially sane.

My humble counsel to anyone who is going to be a caregiver is, for God's sake, the sake of the person you care for, and your own sake, have a few other things in your life. If you don't, caregiving will drain you. And you will come to resent the person you care for. And that will hurt both of you.

I need to say something else about all this. People tell me all the time that I'm a good guy for hanging in here, but they're missing the point. I want to be very clear that this is in my selfish best interest. This isn't selfless stuff I do to support this woman. I have been with her for almost fifty years, and I've got a chance to continue to have her with me in a good-quality-of-life way that I'm not going to sacrifice to a disease that we can beat back together. The very idea that I would have to live without her or watch her decline in front of me is intolerable. So I'm in this game to win it just as much as she is, but I'm in it for me as much as for her. And in a truly selfish sense, maybe more.

Lori and I are very private, so it is difficult for us to tell the world about our darker moments. Life has certainly not been a straight line, and there have been more than a few dark moments. This disease is a teacher, but Lori and I wish we didn't have to learn some of the lessons.

In an earlier chapter, I mentioned the quote from Aeschylus that described how Lori's pain coming to grips with the need to take her medications had helped her learn some very powerful lessons. I often console myself as well with it as I feel it's a remarkable description of our mutual journey. Allow me to repeat: "Even in our sleep, pain which cannot forget falls drop by drop upon the heart until, in our despair, and against our will, comes wisdom through the awful grace of God."

Anne Heynen

Along with several of our mutual friends, we take care of Lori; we drive her, make dinners, and help with different things when she and Bob need it. But Bob has got it on his mind 24/7. I can see the struggle on his face sometimes. I mean, he goes and goes and goes, dealing with it all the time. He does take care of himself by hiring someone to help in certain areas because he's aware of the stress on caregivers, and by taking those critical breaks that restore energy and the right attitude.

Linda Hilton

I first met Lori and Bob right after I returned to the Chicago area from Alaska. It was the summer right after her crisis when Lori was in the same rehab facility as my mother. I soon realized they were really fun to talk to, so I would tell my mom, "Let's take a walk and go visit Bob and Lori in Lori's room." I was starting to look for work just as they were starting to look for help for Lori when she went home. I actually started working for them while she was still in the Mather Home. I would walk down with her to physical therapy and take a walk with her around the ward or lift weights in her room. When she came home from the Mather in August, she was still quite fragile and needed someone around a good bit of the time. She is so much better now, Bob can leave her for a couple of hours to go do what he needs to do without making sure someone is there with her. That would have never happened a year ago.

I make sure she eats healthy meals and that she stays hydrated, as dehydration is a serious problem for Parkinson's patients. If I see her water bottle is half-empty or almost empty, I will say, "You have to drink that before you leave home."

When I stay overnight while Bob is out of town, I tell her she just needs to sit down and rest, but she always tells me she will do it later. If you were to spend three days and nights with her as I have, you would see that she does not stop. She does get a lot of rest at night because she goes to bed at nine and gets up around seven or seven thirty. But during the day, Lori is go, go, go.

Right now, I am mostly her companion and chauffer. I take her on walks and run errands with her, whatever she wants. If she wants to go to the Shores Club to work out, I take her and lift weights with her. What's neat is that she is doing so well she doesn't really need a classic caregiver in the more intense sense any more.

I am paid for fifteen hours a week. Sometimes I work less, sometimes I work more, but it all averages out. I drive her to her regularly scheduled caregivers: Monday to Debbie for massage; Wednesdays we go to Dr. Sha; and Thursday I don't work. Wednesday afternoon, Bob takes her to Feldenkrais® because he takes a lesson too. What's inspiring is when we do our "tour du caregiver." I've been so impressed by how the other caregivers all seem to really care about her too. She's drawn all of us into this fight, and we all want her to win.

Lori

Let's move on to Debbie since I start my calendar week with a deep-tissue massage. Debbie is a friend, but frankly, she's a real pusher, someone I've come to think of as a caring drill sergeant.

Debbie Campbell

I met Lori prediagnosis. She was already having tremors, but she had not yet been diagnosed with Parkinson's.

With this disease, about the time you see tremors, rigidity has already set in. What happens with Parkinson's is that the muscles are actually firing in a disorganized, chaotic fashion all the time. That is why anyone with PD needs to up his or her caloric intake. This is why Lori got so skinny—because the patient doesn't realize, even when he or she is on the medicine and doesn't see the tremors, the muscles are firing all the time.

This is why massage helps. It helps with the rigidity; the less rigid the muscles are, the fewer tremors. When the muscles are rigid, it is hard to move them, so every movement is slower.

Massage really works for Parkinson's patients. If you loosen the muscles, they respond quicker when the person uses them. If you know anything about Eastern medicine, everything is about the meridians, the channels through which the life energy flows. You can heal through the muscles because you affect the meridians.

In the beginning, Lori did a lot of alternative therapies. I recommended homeopathy, nutrition; they all help. We also got her taking tai chi and harp lessons. She was using all of those therapies as well as Parkinson's medicine. Because of everything she was doing, she was able to use minimal Parkinson's medicine for the first ten or twelve years.

Over time we became friends. I don't generally become friends with my clients, but I did with Lori. I knew her from church, and we found out our daughters were friends in college. I am the bad cop—as in good cop/bad cop—partly because she knows how much I love her. I let her know when she is not drinking enough water or doing anything else that threatens her well being. What I do is called compassionate guidance. I am not a therapist, but I can hold her hand and help her think about choices and consequences. I have been doing a lot of that. Sometimes I step outside boundaries and talk to her the way a daughter would.

My first impression of Lori was that she was so beautiful, with such a gracious demeanor. She is very poised. Her inner beauty shines through her eyes. I think this battle has been a journey that in many ways has humbled her. In another way it has made her very angry, an emotion that has fed her determination. But this disease has also taught her so much, just as she has taught the rest of us about how to face an immense challenge.

The girl is just amazing.

Bob

Because we kept searching for the best treatments for Lori, we discovered several alternative therapies. One that we found was the Feldenkrais Method®, with an excellent practitioner named

Cheryl Becker. We thought that might be one more avenue. But you know, it is what you do: you keep looking. Feldenkrais® lessons are incredibly gentle, but very effective. I do it with Cheryl following Lori most weeks, and she has essentially cured my sleep apnea and helped keep my two artificial hips flexible. We're believers. For example, she challenged an exercise Lori was doing on her own where the objective was strength. Cheryl demonstrated how this exercise was actually inhibiting balance. She's a master at integrated therapy, which pulls a lot of the various therapies together—a huge value.

Cheryl Becker

How do I explain Feldenkrais®? First, it is not another type of massage. It isn't a form of chiropractic either. It is a series of lessons developed by Moshe Feldenkrais, a physicist. It started with his trying to conquer his own knee pain. That probably doesn't make it very clear. Let me start by explaining my own encounter with Feldenkrais® because I think that will help you understand it better.

In my yoga class, I was having problems standing on the four points of my feet. I had been trying for years. Someone suggested Feldenkrais® might help, so I went to a practitioner who had me lie down on a table. He lifted my leg, pressed a little into my hip joint, and said, "Can you feel that?" I thought, *Well, is there someone who couldn't feel that?* And he did the same thing to my other leg and then my arms. I thought, *This is probably one of the dumbest things I have ever paid money for.* I didn't think there could be any change, but when I stood up, the four points of my feet went like radar to the ground. I was so impressed that in fifty minutes he could change me into doing something I had been trying on my own for years. I did it without thinking about it. So I decided to read Moshe Feldenkrais's book *Body and Mature Behavior.* It's a study of anxiety, sex, gravitation, and learning. After I went for a second lesson, I thought, *This is something*

I could be good at. I think I would like to do this professionally. It wasn't easy since I couldn't take time off work to spend four years training, as required by the Feldenkrais® method, but eventually I managed.

Moshe Feldenkrais said, "As we become aware of what we are doing in fact, and not what we say or think we are doing, the way to improvement is wide open to us."[3] This has been particularly important for Lori because her sense of where her body was in space often did not match her actual location. To some degree, most people experience this, but I have found it's worse in people with Parkinson's.

I think mostly about the skeleton and the nervous system because I am giving someone what we call a nonverbal conversation with their nervous system. Mostly I am asking questions of your nervous system: How do you feel about this? What would this be for you? What if you felt yourself this way— would you like it? Does this make any sense compared to what I did before?

The lessons teach a person to move more easily. Once she incorporates easier movements into her repertoire, she will naturally use them whenever they are appropriate. For example, whenever we learn something new, such as riding a bicycle, we need to pay attention to how we are moving. After we learn how, we can ride the bike without thinking about it. That is what Feldenkrais® promotes, easier movements without thinking, even though this kind of thinking is nonverbal.

Parkinson's patients often have to think in order to move. For example, he might have to think, *Feet apart, feet apart,* to keep from tripping. Feldenkrais® lessons aim to teach him to move without having to think constantly in words. This will make life easier and safer.

---

[3]   Moshe Feldenkrais, "Mind and Body," *Systematics, The Journal of The Institute for the Comparative Study of History, Philosophy and the Sciences* (1964).

At the end of a lesson, I actually discourage talking because words are linear and limiting. When my clients get up, they feel the whole self in every movement.

I first met Lori October 31, 2000, three years after she was diagnosed. She has come regularly ever since. She and Bob decided to try Feldenkrais® because it teaches movement. While there aren't specific lessons for people with Parkinson's, Lori is not my only client with this disease. What I have seen over many years in Parkinson's patients is a general, slow decline in the ability to tell a difference in the body. In the sensation of weight, for example, you have more weight on one foot than the other. So you are able to tell a difference between the weight on one foot and the weight on the other. You can feel a difference in touch and muscle contraction as well.

I have noticed my clients with Parkinson's have more difficulty than the average person in sensing these differences kinesthetically. I use both words and touch to invite my students to perceive and compare their sensations. This requires a lot of attention and thinking, which Lori has done willingly. Her skill in sensing differences kinesthetically has improved dramatically. If you can't sense the difference, how can you move? Still her path has zigged and zagged. She has learned, forgotten, and relearned. She has fallen and gotten back up many times.

Lori has problems with breathing, with balance, and with movement in general, as well as with vision. We do lessons so that she is able to bend down and reach up and turn and look behind. Lori's vision problems don't have to do with being unable to see but with orientation. For most people, vision is key to orientation—being able to look one direction while you walk in another. It is more difficult for Lori to look away from her feet to tell where she is going, but always looking down is also limiting. Other lessons are organized about everything from being able to sit comfortably to getting out of a chair. Lori has had difficulty getting up from a chair, so we have worked a lot on that. Almost every time we work on balance, I sneak in something about breathing.

For a long time, Lori had to learn how to think in words to slow down. Now she does not have to depend on word reminders as much. Slowing down is tough. I think Parkinson's makes slowing down particularly difficult. Perhaps because of the effort to overcome a feeling of "freezing," people with Parkinson's can appear to lurch when they walk. They also have trouble lifting their feet high enough. Often Lori's feet would lag behind her upper body in her rush to get somewhere; this leads to falls. Thus, to walk without falling, Lori has to coordinate two parts of her brain, where most people only use one part. She also has to keep reminding herself in words to compensate for her kinesthetic difficulty, which is not a word process. In Feldenkrais® lessons, her slower movements give her system enough time to learn movements.

Lori is a remarkable student. Learning takes attention and effort even when you are lying on the table. Learning to tell differences is also a skill that is grown and developed. Many people are embarrassed when they realize they aren't doing what they think they are doing, but Lori just laughs and tries again. Physical abilities are a big part of self-image for most people so they can react quite emotionally to failure of any sort. But Lori doesn't take herself too seriously. Seeing Lori handle her difficulties so matter-of-factly has inspired me to take myself less seriously.

What I would say from all of my working with her is that she is not just better than she was at her worst the summer before last, she is better than she has been in years. Her improvement has been gradual. All the other things she is doing contribute, from playing the harp to golf lessons. She uses what she learns in Feldenkrais® when she does all these other things so they all reinforce each other. If you learn French but never practice speaking, you will never really be able to speak. It is the same idea with Feldenkrais®. It doesn't stop here in my studio with the lessons. Lori practices all the time. It is just amazing how hard she works on all these things.

I take notes on all my clients after each session, and in addition, over the past twelve years I have kept a log of "Lori Patin's Surgeries, Accidents, Difficult Events" (see the appendix).

Reviewing it in preparation for my remarks for the book, I was struck again by her courage and determination. She never complains and never seeks sympathy. She simply gets up and keeps on trying. I noted twenty-four falls, including one that caused her to break her wrist, another that broke her toe, and another in which her head broke through the laundry room wall. In addition to the surgeries to repair her wrist and toe, she has had cataract surgery and a pacemaker installed. She has experienced shortness of breath, fainting, and a precipitous drop in blood pressure. Through all these trials, she maintains her good spirits. Yet the most remarkable thing of all about my log is that I have no new notes since June 2011 because she has not suffered surgery, accident, or any difficult event since then.

She has wonderful attention and wonderful awareness. Most of all she has a wonderful attitude. I admire Lori greatly for all that she has gone through and for all her work toward healing herself. And I admire Bob equally for all his love, support, research, and caregiving for Lori.

Lori

Very much as Cheryl Becker does with Feldenkrais®, Dr. Lixin Sha uses acupuncture to keep the receptors in my nervous system open and working when my brain tries to tell my body what it should be doing and how it should be moving. I have been with her now for about fourteen years.

Dr. Sha puts needles in me from the top of my head to the tip of my toes. She sticks in twenty to thirty needles at a time. Most of the time it doesn't hurt much. Sometimes it does if she hits a point at a nerve ending. Then it is like an electrical shock that goes up my arm. According to Chinese theory, your body has about twenty meridians that are channels of energy—known as chi—and four hundred-some acupuncture points, each of which has a specific purpose. For example, Dr. Sha almost always puts a needle in two points that are located on the meridians or lines of chi that go up and down my arm and into the core of my body. She says she talks to my nervous system and to my brain by maneuvering my body with the needles.

Dr. Sha leaves the pins in for twenty minutes. After she takes them out, I can go home. The needles are tiny, very thin, like your hair. She feels around and knows that she has to be in a certain area. It is not just a tiny point; you have a little allowance as far as location. I see her for ten weeks straight and then I get two weeks off because she doesn't want my body to become too accustomed to the acupuncture.

Debbie Campbell recommended that I visit an acupuncturist. When I first went to see Dr. Sha, I liked her immediately. She is so sweet, so kind, so gentle. She is full of energy and full of life. She just fits me.

Dr. Lixin Sha

I have been practicing acupuncture for thirty years. I studied it for four years in China, graduating from Shanghai University of Traditional Chinese Medicine in 1982. I also earned my medical doctor degree in China. That takes another three years. I came to this country in 1991 when my husband was studying for his PhD in molecular biology at Northwestern University. After I learned English, I began practicing acupuncture here in August 1998. Lori came to me that same year in December, one year after she had received her diagnosis.

When she first came for treatment, besides acupuncture, Lori consulted a nutritionist, a physical therapist, and a massage therapist, as well as taking music lessons. Immediately I could see that she is a very open-minded lady. She exposes herself to everything. She tries very hard to find anything that can help her slow down the disease. When she came to my clinic, I clearly told her acupuncture does help energy, blood circulation, and balance—all key problems to Parkinson's. It also helps general health and well-being.

I was able to tell Lori on that first visit that I think acupuncture helps Parkinson's people a great deal. I also told her I can't promise that I can help her to stop the Parkinson's progression, but I do believe we can improve her condition. The first time she consulted with me, I could tell she was fragile and weak. So that is what we started working on. She responded well after the first course of the treatment, saying, "I feel that my thinking is clearer and my energy is much better. I am able to handle more." So we continued with the treatments. She is such a good patient, very disciplined.

In addition, Lori hardly ever gets sick with a cold or flu. She comes so regularly that as soon as she gets sick, I take care of it by giving her a special treatment and providing herbal medicine that helps keep sickness away if you take it right away.

Lori's approach is almost a kind of therapy in and of itself. Many people stop coming as soon as their energy levels increase, but Lori is not that kind of person. Because she is so disciplined, she keeps at it when she sees results. I have treated many Parkinson's patients, but in Lori I see something else. Her current remission is the most significant I have ever seen. I am so happy that Lori is in remission and that she is doing so well. I think her acupuncture treatment, her massage, her music, and everything she does help her.

The summer before last, I realized she was slipping and told her husband that he might need to eventually get her to the hospital. I think that it was six months before she was actually hospitalized. I noticed she was more fragile and had severe memory loss, as well as trouble breathing. She was falling all the time because she was fainting. It was very scary. I suspected that her medicines were potentially too strong or that she had a problem with an internal organ. At the hospital, they found out it was the combination of medicines that was causing at least part of the problem. They also put in a pacemaker, which helped a lot.

When Lori told me, "Dr. Sha, I have been asked by Bob and others to write about my experience with fighting Parkinson's," I said, "That is great, Lori," and my eyes opened wide because I was so excited. She said, "I have had these problems for so many years and have worked so long and hard that I feel I have something to tell people that may encourage others." And she does. I think she will inspire other people through the telling of her amazing story.

Jen

I had an incredible experience with Dr. Sha when I was pregnant with my third child. I didn't really believe in acupuncture, so I thought Dr. Sha was some kind of "witch doctor." But I had a big problem, and my parents suggested I take it to Dr. Sha. A week before I was due, my baby was transverse and still hadn't turned. My doctor was talking about giving me a C-section because I couldn't go into labor with the baby transverse because it could be life threatening for both of us. I thought, *Oh my God, I can't have a C-section when I have two other little children already.* My youngest at the time was fifteen months and the oldest was four. Then Mom said her acupuncturist told her to bring me in because she could do something for me. I thought, *This is crazy.* But I was desperate, so I said, "Fine. I'll go. We'll try it out and see what happens. Why not? Mom's paying."

After Dr. Sha had me lie down on the table, she put needles in my toes, particularly my two pinkie toes. Then she put heat up to the needle with some kind of cigar-butt thing. It was hot but didn't hurt. Dr. Sha said the pinkie toe has some relation to some organ in my body that would mirror where the baby was and whatever it was doing with that organ would make the baby so uncomfortable that it would move away. So I am lying there with these needles in my toes and the cigar thing next to the needle, thinking, *This is insane.* It went on like this for fifteen minutes, and I never felt a thing.

Then Dr. Sha took all the stuff out and said, "Yes, the baby's right." And I thought, *What? It can't be. I didn't even feel anything.* But it worked; he turned right then and there! In the next few days when I went in for my visit with my OB, she told me the baby had turned. I said, "You are not going to believe this," and told her about Dr. Sha. Of course my OB is a traditional Western doctor, so she said, "Well, we don't know if that is really what caused it." Hey, I was in Dr. Sha's office when it happened. Later when my parents told Dr. Sha how amazed we all were, she said, "Why are you so surprised? This happens in China all the time." One more success story for Eastern medicine. And one more believer.

Bob

One of the other things I find so compelling about Lori's influence is how she has so quietly pulled others into the circle of people dedicated to helping her beat this thing. She's not a John Wayne personality, not an Oprah, not a Garrison Keillor–type storyteller. She just goes about the task in her own quiet, sweet, determined way. What continues to delight me is how Lori has drawn all her caregivers into her struggle until they are all as committed to fighting Parkinson's as she and I are.

The concept "the whole is greater than the sum of the parts" truly applies to Lori's loving caregivers. It's not that they coordinate, but attacking her disease with so many therapies has a halo effect for Lori beyond the individual treatments. And it's not just what they do, it's what they do to trigger in Lori the desire to please them because they deeply care for her at a level that cannot be underestimated or remotely paid enough for—and she responds. Angels do, indeed, not only walk among us, but, in Lori's case, they hover.

CHAPTER 6

Exercise, Diet, and Sleep

IT TAKES MONEY, TIME, AND discipline to do all Lori does, and many people may not have the financial resources to be able to follow a regime like hers. But an enemy as ugly and intransigent as Parkinson's has to be attacked on every possible front with whatever resources a patient can muster. Much can be done without a lot of money. Through the years, she has put together a program that includes diet, exercise, and sleep that anyone with the commitment and attitude can do, which attains the greatest effectiveness in combination with medication.

Exercise is magic. Dr. Rezak concurs. "Exercise and nutrition have clearly helped Lori. We can slow down the disease's progress with exercise and certain medications. I can act on whatever situation comes up with my patients, but the other half of the equation is what the patients do for themselves. There is no question that my patients who do better take the exercise and physical therapy recommendations seriously—and they are in the minority. In my practice, the people who need less medicine are careful about their nutrition, exercise, and go to physical therapy. Their symptoms are milder. They are just better for longer periods of time."

A recent article in the *Chicago Tribune* validated her belief in the power of exercise. Dr. Dennis Keane, a physical medicine and rehabilitation physician at Rush-Copley Medical Center in Aurora, Illinois, thinks a dedicated exercise program will not only control the symptoms of Parkinson's but may slow the disease's progression and possibly even prevent its manifestation. He explains that

89

exercise helps because "our brains have neuroplasticity. That is, with activities such as exercise, we stimulate our brains to create new nerve pathways to take over the role of what we may have lost from a neurological disorder." In fact, he points out recent research that shows exercise also can protect against Parkinson's, both by defending the brain against toxins and by increasing neurochemicals that cause nerves to grow and get stronger and more stable. Dr. Keane says, "This is exciting news, as it is believed that symptoms of Parkinson's disease do not manifest until one loses 40 to 60 percent of their nerve function. Perhaps with exercise, those at risk will not have symptoms until later in life or perhaps never at all."[4]

Lori

This is what I call good news. I am getting back on the treadmill now.

Jen

When I think about Mom's remission from Parkinson's, I know it has to be largely attributed to her tenacity. When she first found out she had the ugly disease, she said, "I must challenge this and am going to explore every avenue to do so." She just tried everything and stuck with things that worked, and many of those have really helped her. I think if she didn't do all that she does with diet, exercise, and sleep, it would certainly be a different story. It would be a different book that we would be writing.

---

[4]   Bonnie Miller Rubin, "Exercise Found to Alleviate Symptoms of Parkinson's Disease," *Chicago Tribune*, December 19, 2012.

When my mother got her diagnosis, she started putting a whole lot more attention and focus on what she had to do herself as the primary owner of both the problem and the solution.

Bob

When I think of Lori's diet, exercise, and sleep regimes as central parts of her battle, I think in terms of Maslow's Pyramid of Human Needs. Abraham Maslow was a twentieth-century humanist psychologist who believed that man—or woman—lives life based on a hierarchy of specific needs that build upon each other. You can't move on to a higher level unless the levels beneath have been met. The most basic level is food, water, elimination, sleep—basic health—and after that comes safety. When these needs are met, you then can seek love and belonging, and then self-esteem. The highest level of the pyramid is self-actualization, where you finally become the person you were capable of being, and not everyone who meets the earlier levels even strives for the pinnacle. In Lori's situation, it's a great way for me to think about both how she faces her disease and how someone else might face any big challenge.

At her lowest point, Parkinson's undermined Lori's most basic needs. While she had food and beverages available, she was often not physically able to eat or drink enough. We constantly asked her, do you have enough to eat? Can you hydrate? Can you go to the bathroom? Moreover, overly vivid dreams kept her from getting a good night's sleep. These are all part of the very foundation of human life. Now she is able to eat and hydrate sufficiently. Her basic bodily functions perform well, and she sleeps as well as someone can with the REM sleep disorder. As to the next level, often she was simply not safe. Oftentimes she wasn't even able to walk very far without falling down. Now her balance is so much better that her safety is not in question as it was before. And even when reasonably safe, she started thinking about the ability to connect with others. Is she mobile enough? Can she communicate? Can she write? Can she talk? Can she even interact? All these are so important to being in her comfort zone.

In terms of the Pyramid of Human Needs, Lori now does quite well with the basic needs as well as the love, belonging, and relationship levels. Her core needs are being met, with very few exceptions. Her relationships are firm and sustaining; she knows the two of us have something there that certainly may not be perfect but is essentially concrete and supportive.

Then the effort to gain control enters. When you don't have a reasonable level of control over your life and you aren't even really safe, you can feel helpless and easily fall into a negative spiral. So all the exercise and therapies come into play because she is trying to attack this problem from all sides to gain physical control, which helps lead to emotional control. As I've thought about this through the eyes of her unique situation, I think control is really a critical part of not only each of the lower levels but certainly of self-actualization.

While the metaphor might not be perfect, Maslow's Pyramid of Human Needs resembles the hill that Lori is climbing with Parkinson's. She is striving for that last level where she enters the rare space where she becomes all that she can be, given the limitations of the challenge she faces. But it doesn't matter if she actually gets there. She gets as close as she can every day, and that's enough.

Lori

When I was diagnosed with Parkinson's, even my eating patterns changed because I needed to put on weight. The summer before I went into the comas, I wasn't getting enough to eat or drink. I was down to ninety-four pounds. I have put on fifteen pounds since then. Aly tells me, "One of the most important things you accomplished was the change in your diet. Because you concentrated on your nutrition, you are much more substantial and have more energy."

I also have an allergy to wheat and gluten, and that is just the way I am; this is not because of Parkinson's. I have had problems with my stomach since I was young. It never took much for me to get a stomachache. Nevertheless, my stomach problems intersect with Parkinson's because it is important for me to keep my weight up. Even though I was always kind of careful of what I ate, I had no idea how bad wheat and corn are for me. For breakfast, I would have a piece of toast. I wouldn't feel good in the morning so I wouldn't eat right away. Then I would drink orange juice and eat the piece of toast. That toast was killing me, although I didn't know it. I still didn't feel good, so as a result, I would eat another piece. After that I felt even worse, and that was my day. I ate as many wheat- or gluten-based carbohydrates as I possibly could even though it was the worst thing for me to eat.

I finally figured out my problem by going to a local nutritionist, Bonnie Minsky, who had helped a friend of mine who had breast cancer. After a barrage of chemo treatments, my friend lost her appetite, was not eating, and as a result was wasting away. The nutritionists said my friend was allergic to wheat and gluten and needed to radically change her diet. She needed to get off everything that had gluten in it—which is a lot. It is not easy to give up everything with wheat and corn in it. Corn does not have gluten, but it bothers my stomach. However, when my friend did it for two weeks, she started to feel better and gain weight.

Another friend had told me to read books by Andrew Weil, MD, because they might give me some further clues to a diet that would make me feel better. So I read a couple of Weil's books, such as *8 Weeks to Optimum Health,* and did other research on dietary implications for my symptoms. It all reinforced my feeling that my allergy to wheat and gluten was undermining my own constitution and making the Parkinson's worse. I worked with the nutritionist for ten years and have been maintaining my gluten-free diet ever since. I have to eliminate all grains, wheat, barley, everything but rice. If a food has rice only in it, it is okay. Also, no corn, cornstarch, or corn syrup because these bother me. That means no processed foods. Processed foods are terrible for me because they put corn syrup in almost all of them. Now after ten years of a gluten-free diet, I can eat things with corn syrup, but only moderately. Now I feel great. Food has become an ally.

The gluten-free diet has made a big difference but didn't solve everything diet-wise overnight. I do know some people on this diet who have lost a lot of weight because, in the past, it had no baked goods or breads. It was all fruit and vegetables and meats. Meats are excellent and very important. You can have some grains, like brown and wild rice. Cheese is good too, and I eat a lot of it. In the last few years, the gluten-free diet has become very popular and much better supported with bakery products. Now there are gluten-free stores that sell not just produce but cookies, donuts, cereals, English muffins, and bagels, all gluten-free. They all taste the same as regular baked goods for the most part. Now even the local grocery stores carry a lot of gluten-free products.

In addition, I try to hydrate like crazy. Drinking enough water is critical, and Parkinson's patients, for some unknown reason, often forget to hydrate, with negative consequences. And I also take salt tablets to help me retain water and support my naturally low blood pressure. I am even supposed to eat a bag of potato chips or a substitute every day. Some people would feel lucky if a doctor told them they had to eat that many chips. I do it out of obligation. Poor me!

Aly

Mom is now so much steadier and stronger and beefed up. She is the heaviest I have ever seen her. She has always been thin, and thin people tend toward osteoporosis. People with Parkinson's fall a lot, and Mom has been no exception. If she falls, even somewhat gently, she can easily break a bone. That is always the scariest part for me, the falling.

When we were growing up, my mom was the "Energizer Bunny." She was always active, athletic, running. In fact, she was an aerobics teacher when we were growing up. She would run down to the post office just for the joy of it. She was just always going and going and going and was very fit. Mom tried to be health conscious with what she ate, except when we were little— she still drank a two-liter bottle of Diet Coke a day, and certain foods seemed to upset her stomach a lot. All my friends would say, "You have such a healthy mom." That was certainly the image of her in my head. Never in your wildest dreams would you think that she might someday have something like Parkinson's, which would rob her of so many things that she enjoyed and that made her who she was.

Lori

For someone like me who used to be so physically fit, it is no chore to exercise. Walking on the treadmill or lifting weights come easily to me. What is most difficult for me is ordinary walking and sitting. I have to be very conscious of how I am performing these everyday activities that should be so simple. When I walk, I have to think to keep my legs apart or my feet have a tendency to hit each other. I also have to remember to keep my back straight, not to shuffle. And despite all my best efforts, Bob says I sometimes stoop. To remind me in public, he's developed this little phrase, "SUS," which means "stand up straight." Another thing, I have a tendency to lean to the left as my brain tells me that left leaning is normal when it's not. I need to tell myself to lean toward the right so that I basically stand and sit straight. I have been trying to move more slowly when I walk. If I try to catch up with someone who is walking fast, I am a goner. The same with sitting: I have to be very careful how I stand up. I have always been a very "got-to-get-up-and-do-this" kind of person, so all of a sudden having to take more time to get up and move is driving me crazy. I've had to learn that speed is not my friend.

There are a lot of things I used to enjoy that I can't do anymore. I can't ride a bike, ski, or roller blade anymore. But I have started playing golf again. I played golf for two years before

I got really sick, and now I am playing again—that's how much better I am. I hit a short, straight ball. I just want to get back to where I was before I was sick, not good but not holding anyone up. Bob is really proud of me for coming back. He says, "When you just see Lori walk unassisted up to the tee and swing the club, you see proof of how far she's come back."

I don't do exercises just for my body, I do them for my voice and face too. People with Parkinson's tend to speak very softly and lose facial expression. You would laugh if you walked into my house and heard me doing my voice exercises in the next room. They used to scare the dog, but now he thinks that screeching and grunting are just more weird human habits.

I also have exercises that I do for my face because the face of a Parkinson's patient tends to become rigid and expressionless. They even have an expression for it—the mask of Parkinson's. And I don't want that to happen to me. Who has a grandma who never smiles? I got my facial exercises from my mother, who found a European book of facial exercises to do instead of a facelift. And they work. And Bob says that is a double benefit as I look normal and we don't have any money leftover anyway for plastic surgery.

I also do exercises to improve my memory because even though I don't have Alzheimer's, I have a memory that is not as acute as it used to be. For example, when I came back from the hospital, there were words I couldn't pull out of my head. It was frightening. For instance, I couldn't come up with the word "carriage." I struggled and struggled. Then I got it. Once I got it, I never had a problem remembering it again. Well, that can do a job on your vocabulary and your confidence. So to exercise my memory I play bridge every week for three hours at a time. And that has helped a lot because there is so much memory in the game.

When I was in the hospital, someone brought me Sudoku, a game of number patterns. That's good for your memory too. I do more reading than I used to, which also helps me with words I can't come up with. I also went to a store called Marbles, which sells games, mental exercises, and other tools for your mind.

I bought a memory game that is about an art auction where different things are auctioned off and they are all pre-priced. You have to remember what the pre-price was and what the final auction price was. All these may not protect my ability to function intellectually, but they surely seem to help. And you know what? They're fun. I've learned that if I can make mental exercises fun, I'm far more likely to do them.

I believe passionately in exercise as critical to my crusade against Parkinson's. I have always loved to work out, but when I was really sick, I couldn't. My arms were so tired I couldn't lift them. Today I am back to my exercise regime. I stretch every morning. Then I walk outside or on the treadmill for a half hour every day. I ride a stationary bike for a half hour three times a week. Most nights I do a little tai chi or maybe a few ballroom dancing moves for balance. In tai chi, you are always in motion, but you are always trying to stay relaxed, and balance is key to that. My evidence that tai chi works is that, if I have a massage after a lesson, Debby can get her fingers right down to the bone. At home almost every day, Bob and I do additional balance exercises in which he stands behind me and shoves and pushes me while making sure I don't fall. This helps me practice reacting to situations where I might be bumped or start to trip and have to save myself from falling.

As exercise for my fingers and my mind, I play the harp twenty minutes a day. Physically your fingers are in opposition because all your fingers are working, not only the finger that pulls but all the others too. My harp instructor says I am using my fingers in ways I couldn't have done two years ago. I also came up with the harp as my own therapy. I have since learned that the harp is good for many neurological functions because the vibrations are so good for you. The harp vibrates and rests against your body, so you feel it throughout your body and brain. There is a program called Healing Harps, a harp institute at Southern Illinois University. They found playing the harp helped people who had neurological disorders. The harp creates a series of vibrations that create energy flow that travels into the brain just like chi, and that seem to support neurological connections. I'll never be a good harpist, but I love my teacher and the effort as it makes music in my body, which makes music in my mind and maybe also in my soul.

Then I do weights again in the afternoon. I used to work with a trainer, but I pushed myself too hard and got hurt, so I've learned to limit both the weight and the number of repetitions. It's just a constant set of adjustments to what your body will let you do without harming yourself.

I'm also kind of proud that I am the one who thought up doing tai chi and ballroom dancing for balance. They are both great fun, and Bob willingly goes with me although he isn't flexible enough to do some of the tai chi moves and his basic cha-cha is almost laughable.

Linda

I am twenty years younger, but I have a hard time keeping up with her. She still wants to life weights and do balance exercises and stuff when I'm ready for TV.

Lori

I need a really good night's sleep so I often go to bed at nine. It's not even dark in the summer. I try to get eight to nine hours a night. If I get eight hours, I am in fine shape but nine is luxury. I take a half hour to finally get up, so I try to wake up slowly and start flexibility exercises in bed. When I get up really slowly, then I am also less likely to have breathing or balance problems as the day begins.

As with most people, I am not fully rested if I don't get enough REM sleep, and as you already know, I do some pretty funny things during that deep-sleep stage. Bob told you earlier about how people with Parkinson's often physically act out their dreams.

These REM sleep disturbances have had a big effect on our going to the movies. The only kind of movie I will go see is a comedy or a romance. No drama or anything with violence and blood. I hate them because they give me nightmares. Bob used to discount the impact until I would have a nightmare and wake him up shaking or hitting him whenever I saw a blood-and-guts movie. So he decided that a movie that stimulates his testosterone level is just not worth it.

Bob

As I think about some of the central themes in Lori's story over all these years, certainly the theme of buying time comes to mind. What she does every day is earn some additional hours, days, weeks, months, or even years for research to emerge that will create positive developments to prolong her quality of life. Maybe even a cure. Just recently, the *Chicago Tribune* published a story about just the type of research we are hoping for: "A Northwestern University researcher said they have created compounds that could slow the effects of Parkinson's disease."[5]

It's also a story about using time for the things that both matter and add purpose.

One more theme that I'd heard before, but seems to be fully resonant with this story, is what a lot of older people say, "If you rest, you rust." This is particularly true for Parkinson's patients. I'm often amazed in the evening when I'm ready to simply veg out, and Lori says it's time to do her balancing exercises. She drags me into the process when I'd just as soon sit on my butt on the couch and watch a ballgame. It's a form of leadership in a real sense when

---

[5] Jessica Tobacman, "NU Reports Progress in Brain Care," *Chicago Tribune*, February 6, 2013, Section 5, 5.

she has to manage the resources around her, including her hubby, when they would just as soon pack it in.

For a while, I had to hold her up to dance. Now she is back doing the ballroom dancing moves of years ago. I'm sure you can imagine her joy. Imagine my joy in tagging along.

CHAPTER 7

❦

Spirituality and Attitude

LORI TRULY BELIEVES SHE IS a lucky person in an unlucky situation. In spite of Parkinson's, her life has been blessed and perhaps explained best in a quote from Romans 5: "Suffering produces endurance. Endurance produces character. Character produces hope. And hope does not disappoint." She has a strong and personal relationship with God that is fundamental to her fight against Parkinson's. She maintains a positive attitude in this struggle, which she believes God's grace, in all of its manifestations, has allowed her.

Lori

The Church of the Holy Comforter is the anchor to our spiritual life, although I consider faith as personal and something both within and yet well beyond church. Still, we are lucky that we found our Episcopal church so soon after we moved to Chicago. It is a marvelous church on so many levels and a big part of our lives.

By way of background on how we got to "Holy C," Bob was raised a hardcore Catholic (altar boy at eight), and I was raised a sort-of Lutheran. My family didn't go to church much while I was growing up, but Bob was in his about seven days a week, starting with Mass every school day. Early in our married life we joined the Episcopal church after I had "attempted" to become a Catholic. We were married in the Catholic church because it meant a lot to Bob's family. In those days, when you got married in the Catholic church, you also had to put it in writing that you would raise your children Catholic. Even though I had no intention of doing that, I signed the commitment because Bob really wanted me to do it to appease his family, and, as he often said, "To get you and me into the rack."

For almost a year we went to evening classes so I could learn to be a good Catholic. We met a couple of younger priests, and the classes were going well enough for me . . . until we got to the pope and male-only priests. There were many things about the Catholic religion that I had trouble with, but papal infallibility (the idea that the pope was truly infallible in matters of faith and morals and could not make a mistake) was the first real sticking point. Not having female priests was the second. As I recall, the dialogue went something like this:

L: So. Who told the pope he was infallible and couldn't make a mistake?

B: God, apparently. And the mistakes he can't make only relate to matters of faith and morals, not everyday mistakes like errors in the papal checkbook.

L: Really? Is there, like, a heavenly memo on that? A deposition maybe with God on one side and maybe Abe Lincoln as a lawyer on the other? Maybe God's thumbprint on the document?

B: I don't like where this is going.

L: I don't care. Let's dig deeper, shall we, into, say, matters of morals? Were there any popes in charge during the various inquisitions when people were tortured and killed to save their souls?

B: I don't know; wasn't there. My torture is this discussion.

L: I understand your discomfort. But assuming the inquisition happened as evidenced by historical accounts, could that have been possibly a moral mistake?

B: Maybe.

L: Good. Now that that's settled, let's move on to the issue of women priests.

B: Oh, boy.

L: Why no women priests?

B: Apparently, the guys don't think they're ready. You know, it's the pope and the cardinals who vote on stuff like this.

L: So no women get to vote on the role of women. Why not?

B: Because if they did, the guys would not be in charge. These are not stupid men.

L: Really? So how are women not ready?

B: Don't have a clue. Maybe they need more training.

L: Training from whom?

B: The guys.

L: If I wanted to be a priest, do you think I'd need a lot of training?

B: Nope.

L: Do you think I'd be ready soon?

B: Yes, you'd be ready in seconds. As a matter of fact, you're likely ready right now.

L: Excellent. Looks like we've handled this nicely, and it also seems to me like we're also ready to move on to a new church, right?

B: Yes, dear.

Meanwhile, Polly, his sister, who is a year older than Bob and who got married the year before we did, was experiencing the same dilemma with her husband. She was a Catholic and he was a nonchurchgoer. Polly said, "You know, we have found the Episcopal church works for us. Maybe it would work for you." Right down the street from us in Farmington, Connecticut, was a tiny Episcopal church, St. James. We immediately liked the rector, and the church was well attended with families of all ages. Soon after we started going, we thought, *This is the place for us. This is our "come to the middle" answer. The service is very similar to the Catholic service. Just no infallible pope. And female priests. Catholic "light."*

Nevertheless, the Catholic church has had a deep influence on the way Bob thinks. As Polly says, "Even though my brother and I both left the Church, I think most of our moral thinking comes from being effectively conditioned, in a largely good way, as a Catholic. No, you never lose that, and that's a very good thing."

My feeling is, faith is personal. Each person has his or her unique outlook and personal take. I know Bob's spiritual life is entirely different from mine. That is perfectly all right. It's not a problem for either of us, and I will let him tell you about his faith.

I consider the Bible, for example, a great conglomeration of stories told just as if you were a gypsy and you had important stories with critical moral lessons for your kids and family that you could tell around the campfire. Every time a different person told the story, it might be a little different, but the moral survived. I think it is a great piece of literature. The stories can be quite compelling. Some are very boring or not very believable; some are very believable; and with some it is easy to find parallels with your own life and something that has happened to you. It's the best-selling book in history, and there is a good reason for that.

But as for reading the Bible, I can just as easily sit and look at the flowers in my garden and pray because something miraculous happened after I put a seed in the ground. They are miraculous to me. To look at them is to pray. I pray all the time. I pray for family and friends, for those in trouble, for an end to the evil in the world. And I have all kinds of prayer groups praying for me all the time too. I believe in prayer and so do they.

I feel that if something is right, it will happen. And if it doesn't happen then there is some reason beyond my knowing for it not happening. However, that does not mean I can explain why, halfway across the world, people are killing each other. You think about events in the entire world, and you wonder, *What, in God's or anyone else's name, is happening?* And even here, what is happening when the schools are full of drugs and gangs? When kids just kill each other? When, to be able to be respected in the gang, they have to go out and kill two girls? Something has got to change. Something has to shake us to our roots so we spring up again transformed for the better.

On a spiritual level, being able to reach out to others has been a gift to me. As the St. Francis prayer says, "It is in giving that we receive." So, reaching out to people by writing this book is part of my spiritual journey. I get a lot of phone calls from people who have talked to people who know me. They say, "Do you mind if I have so-and-so call you because they have Parkinson's? They just got diagnosed, and they want to know what they can do." The most recent phone call was from a good friend whose husband still thinks he has a problem with his back even though a doctor has told him the problem is Parkinson's. I know he is not doing any of the exercises or other therapies. Maybe if I write something, it will help him. Maybe it will give him a gentle reminder. Maybe people could keep my book handy so they can look through and see what I try and see if something might work for them. If just one person was inspired to fight harder to conquer his or her own unique challenge, it would all be worthwhile.

I have been so blessed by going into remission. I have the feeling God wants me to do something with this. I shouldn't just turn my back and move on. In my contract with Parkinson's, I have added a clause that says I must pass on the lessons I have learned.

Who was I before PD? I was the same except now I am calmer, more accepting. I am not fatalistic. I am at peace. I am not scared. I feel blessed. Even with all that I have had to give up, I have gained much and have learned more.

Bob

Our faith and our church are important weapons in our arsenal that we both use to fight PD.

Lori may be more grounded in her beliefs than I am, and her faith is real and deep and her very own. Also, her connections to friends are important to her spiritual life. In many respects she has created a unique system of support for herself at Holy Comforter. That is one reason we have gone to this church for some twenty years and will stay there until we croak.

Now if you were to say to Lori—I think it would be an interesting question—"What do you believe?" I am not sure Lori could fully articulate what she believes because it's so uniquely hers and so nuanced to her own evolving self. I think it involves a sense that there must be something guiding our ways. I think her faith comes from an inner belief that there is in fact something more important, something larger than we are. And if you have that broad a belief, maybe you don't have to be rigidly precise about your faith. Maybe it's just there and evolving. As time marches on, it has to be seen through the prism of a whole new set of conditions.

One of our irreverent friends says the Catholics have Ten Commandments, but Episcopalians have Six Commandments and Four Suggestions. I'm still in favor of all ten, but we Episcopalians seem to live with doubt a bit more easily. That's why Lori is comfortable with the Episcopal church, in my opinion. Whether it's a church, a temple, or a mosque, all religions believe God is love and that we should love our neighbor as ourselves.

I struggle with doubts more than Lori does, but I'm somewhat comforted by thinking that doubt is, at least for me and for some others I know, part of a thinking faith. We all have to find a way to either put our doubts to rest or to live with them. But the key will be not what we necessarily say we believe but what our behavior actually proves. I'm forthright about having no clue about some of this, about not being smart enough to figure out the mystery.

But the one thing I'm confident about is that my personal faith has everything to do with belonging. Although I am a true mongrel with Irish, French, and Scottish blood, it is the Scottish gene that calls to me and especially the concept of belonging to a clan. In all faiths, we are called to belong to the ultimate clan—the family of God. We bring all our strengths and weaknesses, our joys and fears, our faith and doubt, and we are welcome. We wish to belong, and in our wishing, we do belong.

At Holy Comforter I became involved in a men's fraternity that met early Friday mornings to talk about what it is to be a man in today's world. At each session, men were encouraged to tell their life stories in terms of the issues in their lives. One session that meant a lot to everyone was called "blood in the water." This is a metaphor for being vulnerable and telling the real story of your life as much as you can stomach the truth. The challenge was to be "honest at a gut level" about your evolution and how it brought you to where you are in your life and spiritual journey. To draw out each man's story, we used the metaphor of a tapestry to present the paradigm. In the front hall, we all hang a tapestry of who we are. It represents the story of our lives as told in the glowing colors of our accomplishments, our victories and ourselves shown in our best light, as we'd like to be perceived. However, right behind the first tapestry, covered up by the illusion of the first, is the real tapestry, full of the vulnerable vignettes of our real lives with successes and failures, doubts alongside deeply held beliefs, the mistakes we've made which have shaped our lives, the worn and frayed aspects of who we really are. It's the real but often hidden story of our hero's journey. These life stories were really hard to deliver. Yet, as we heard each tale, it encouraged others to be forthcoming about whom they really are. Bonds were created that will last for years, perhaps forever, and to me, that's spirituality.

Now, I know from living with the girl for almost fifty years that Lori is hooked on some unique drugs, and they're clearly connected. While there are a lot of pharmaceuticals involved in her care, no pharmacy could ever sell her the most powerful drugs: faith, hope, tenacity, determination, and persistence, all drugs produced by the brain. Lori is a drug addict of the best kind because she generates these drugs herself. On the other hand, and just to showcase that she isn't actually perfect yet, there is still a little bit of "denial drug" mixed into her brain pharmacy. That is why she still does stuff like walk down the steps carrying heavy items in both hands. She doesn't really forget that this is dangerous for her; she just thinks she's fine, so no problem. I look at these as little evasions caused by optimism, not deliberate denials. But I yell at her anyway.

Of all the self-produced drugs, we love hope the best. As long as you have hope, you will be willing to pay whatever price it costs to hang on. That is the beautiful psychology of hope. When hope disappears, that is the turning point psychologically and emotionally. A person without hope takes the attitude of "I am packing it in, why bother, there is no upside here." On Lori's desk in her office, there is a cartoon with a picture of a stork and a frog. The stork has the head of the frog in his mouth and the frog has its hands choking the stork's neck. The caption reads: "Don't ever give up."

Hope needs to be nurtured. There have to be concrete reasons why you have hope. That is why Lori and I pay attention to research, and that is why we go to Parkinson's seminars.

Another reason we go is a sort of strange and awkward and embarrassing blessing. We go because she can see other people with Parkinson's, some of them quite advanced. While that is depressing, and our hearts go out to them, she also looks at herself in that setting and says with gratitude, "I am not there yet; and maybe I don't have to go there." It is the comparison that says, "On one hand I hate where I am going. This thing really isn't curable and it's progressive. I may be like that someday, but I must have hope that I can, with the help of others, still beat this thing. And maybe I can also provide hope to some others with this disease, so they too can beat this thing."

What I've learned in this journey is that hope drives behavior, and good results from the right behaviors drive more hope. It's a positively reinforcing cycle.

Part of hope is the also the idea that you can actually buy time. If you have hope for a future cure, you make a commitment to do the things that buy time so you can make it to that future. What is it that allows her to buy time? It is everything Lori does. In fact, I think the answer is: There is no simple or single approach. You can't rely on any one thing, not the meds, the therapists, the exercise regime, the prayer. You have to be willing to try, to experiment, to go the full 360.

One other way we learn as much as possible is by belonging to Parkinson's organizations and reading medical newsletters. Recently *The Mind Health Report* newsletter had two articles that confirmed our deepest beliefs. In the first, Dr. Paul Nussbaum writes, "I have been a clinician for over 20 years. During that time, I have often seen the effects of positive attitude, compassion, forgiveness and love in treating disease. The difference is that I do not shake my head in disbelief. In fact, I am a strong advocate for the human capacity to heal if we can flood our bodies with the type of positive feelings that produce miracles."[6] In a second piece in the same issue, Dr. Harold Koenig says, "The power of prayer does more than lift your spirits—it can actually heal your body. Recent scientific studies have concluded that a strong spiritual belief system can make you healthier and happier, and help you live longer."[7]

One other theme that has emerged for me through all Lori's battles against her disease is that she's all about beating the unbeatable. Maybe the doctors tell her Parkinson's is progressive and incurable, but way down deep inside, she's not buying that. Mortimer Adler of the Chicago School of Psychology said, "If your original assumptions are wrong, all other decisions compound the mistake."[8] If she were to buy into the assumption that Parkinson's is a lost cause and it's just a matter of time until it gets her, then she would have the tendency to submit to it. If her assumption is that it can be beaten, then she behaves as if she is going to live to be cured. Even if she is wrong, she has pushed the end game off and increased the joy of the game in the meantime. Her attitude is totally consistent with what Yogi Berra said: "It ain't over till it's over."

What else can I say about her? Lori and I are very different from each other, but our relationship has worked, somehow, for a

---

6   Dr. Paul Nussbaum, "Positive Attitude is the Best Treatment," *The Mind Health Newsletter* 6 (June 2012): 4.

7   Dr. Harold Koenig, "Ask the Doctors," *The Mind Health Newsletter* 6 (June 2012): 8.

8   "Health Care Reform: Hearing before the Committee on Energy and Commerce," Part 4, US Congress, House, 1994, 278.

long time. I am much more open with my emotions; she is more private, more introspective. She is heavily grounded in an internal, close-in world. While I respect and love all that, I am more attracted to and grounded in the external world. We both love humor, but even our senses of humor are different. She has a very good sense of humor, but hers is a little drier than mine. Mine's more provocative, and I will provoke humor because I think it is one good way to build relationships. When she builds friendships, she builds them through friendliness, caring, and maybe a little bit more serious aspect of communication than dry humor. I would build a friendship both with seriousness and humor from the outset. Maybe that's why she's said so often, "Bob, those are new people in our lives, and you need to wait a bit before saying some of this stuff."

In some powerful ways she is tougher than anybody I have ever known. For starters, by God, you don't mess with her family. If you do she'll attack, and people are stunned by the aggressiveness of this gentle soul. Lori will hold our family together at all cost. And she is much tougher than I would be with something like Parkinson's. On a scale of 1 to 10 for toughness, I might delude myself into thinking I'm an 8.7, but Lori is a 28. Thankfully we're really both pretty good together at toughing out whatever fate throws at us. We can live with stuff for a long time, but there comes a time and place when we are not going to live with it anymore. We were almost there last summer. That was the darkest moment for us. And she was tougher than all of us put together.

Something else that inspires me is that through all her struggles with Parkinson's, Lori continues to set new goals. For one example, one night recently she said to me, "You and I are going to become great cha-cha dancers." While my internal reaction is that she has a much better chance of doing that than I do, having goals is also part of her spiritual formula because a positive, can-do attitude is so important but also so intangible, just like faith. It is so hard to write about. Yet it underlies everything Lori is and does.

What makes Lori different from so many people? We've all said it in many ways. Stubbornness, determination, refusal to give up, tenacity, hope. And maybe one more thing. She really, really hates her disease. This is not a friend. Divorcing it would be her second-best day. Strangling it in the town square would be her first.

Aly

Mom is one of those rare women who are strong and who deal with whatever they are given. They somehow make it work. I think it probably comes from her growing up, from her ancestry. Whether it's a good thing or a bad thing, they just suck it up. They just don't give way to emotions; they just suck them up and work through things.

One thing I can say that has changed since Mom has been diagnosed is Mom and Dad's connection to church. This has always been a constant for them but never as big a part of their life as it is now. I think their church is their support system because of that sense of family and the spirituality and the sustenance from their clergy and particularly their priest friend, Bob Myers. Holy Comforter is also a big part of their social network. Perhaps because I am older, I am now able to see better how it is influencing them as well as what a gift it is to have in their life.

Jen

I think Mom's remission can be attributed in large part to her tenacity. You know, when she first found out she had Parkinson's, she said, "I am going to fight this, and I am going to change this, and I am going to explore every avenue." She tried everything and stuck with the things that worked. I think that has really helped her. I think if she didn't do all that she does, it would be a different book that we would be writing. I see her as headstrong and fighting. You can tell she has a focus. She really throws herself head first into fighting this disease. She has changed almost everything about her life to do so.

I just remember first seeing a change in her after she was diagnosed. She became so motivated and dedicated to do what she had to do for herself, which was a pretty cool thing to see. We had known for a long time that she is a strong woman, but to see her so focused about herself was something new.

Writing this book is part of her plan. For so long, Mom has had people asking her about what she does to fight Parkinson's, wanting to know how she does it. It will be great to put her story out there.

Chuck and Jeanne Johnson

Chuck: You've got to factor in one more thing about Lori. Factor in the attitude.

Jeanne: She has had a very full life and still does, within the confines of Parkinson's. It used to be a more physical, more adventurous life. Yet she is joyful in spite of it.

Anne and Tom Heynen

Anne: Lori has the best attitude. She has mental toughness. You couldn't do what she does with a bad attitude. She has always been very open about her Parkinson's, yet she has never appeared to us to want sympathy. She's got a smile on her face all the time. Lori doesn't complain about anything.

Lori has told me that many people have called her since her wonderful turnaround after last summer. She told me, "People want to know what I did. 'How did you do it?' It is not because of one thing, it is because of a commitment to do many things. It requires your ability to stay with it and not give up, and it is not easy." She has been an inspiration to me.

Bob and Lori's story is a love story. In church, before her
turnaround, walking up the aisle to take communion, he would
hold tight to her hand. Lori was much worse then, so when she
walked down the aisle, she was just all over the place. When she
came down the steps from communion, half the time she wouldn't
even try to go over and get the railing to help herself down. Yet he
would let her, standing watchful to catch her if she should fall.

You can easily see the enormous love Bob has for Lori. He is
casual in manner and down to earth. He is a kind and good man.
All these qualities are an inspiration. We admire him in many
respects. We admire his business sense. He can be very offbeat;
he can be jovial. Yet when he stands up in front of the church to
talk about something, you see how deep and how thoughtful is his
faith.

Tom: Bob is a very, very spiritual guy. He almost seems
flippant about a lot of things, but when you get past that, he is a
serious, intellectual, spiritual man. More spiritual than intellectual.
He is a fine person, a very good person, and an extremely loyal
husband.

Tom and Judi Hamilton

Tom: Lori trusts. She trusts in Bob. She trusts in herself. And
she has every confidence that this too will pass. There has never
been a moment that she has said, "I'll be stopped by this or I
will have to give up." Instead she says, "We are going to have to
approach this a little bit differently than we did yesterday, but it
will pass. It is just going to take a little longer to figure out the
route." That is the way she approaches Parkinson's. It is just
amazing.

My observation is that both of them have deep religious faith,
but Lori and Bob each have a faith that is specific to her or him. I
know Lori and Bob have each come to her or his own definition, a
belief system that is solid for each of them. I am sure of that.

Lori and Bob are so genuine and basic. They never lose focus on their relationship. This is their very basis.

As far as what they do about fighting Parkinson's, they never get emotional about the disease. They just treat it.

Judi: It doesn't stop them living. It is obviously a big part of their lives, but they just deal with it. The glass is never half-empty. It is always half-full. That is how they look at life. They just keep going. When you think you are having a bad day, think about how they approach the challenges of their lives. They are role models.

Dr. Sha

Scientists are working on a cure for Parkinson's. My husband is a medical biologist, so I know there is hope. Lori said to me, "I am doing everything I can to maintain myself as healthy as possible, because who knows, someday stem-cell therapy may come and bring a cure. There is hope."

Lori

Bob Myers, our longtime and recently retired rector at Holy Comforter is a wonderful, brilliant man. We have known him as long as we have lived in Chicago—twenty years. He retired two years ago, but he still lives close by and we see him often.

Bob

One of our best friends is the former rector of our church, an Episcopal priest and a clinical psychologist. Bob Myers has known us for years and knows us on a level most people don't. And he's watched this Parkinson's struggle since it began.

Bob is a most unusual and gifted man. He has a unique perspective on life and faith that Lori and I certainly agree with.

His insights as a clinical psychologist give him a special depth not often seen in a person of the cloth. He's one of the few people I regard as a master of his profession and a true, total human being.

Bob Myers

When I sat with Lori and Bob to talk about writing this book, the first question I asked was, whose story is it? In my experience, it is not just her story or his story but their story. In spiritual terms, it is the family's issue with Parkinson's, not the individual's.

The second thing I asked them was, "What is it about?" When I read a good book and put it down, I say, "That was a good book; it had a message." My late wife would say, "What was it about?" I think it is important for Lori and Bob, even if they struggle at this point, to decide what this book is about. That will help when they write the story. That comes from my professional experience in doing sermons.

In my opinion, on the deepest level, it is about a love story. It is a story of love between a man and a woman who face life's adversities. It is in the context of a much bigger life journey. It is a story of love between two people who passionately care about one another and who refuse to give in. And it is a love that is not defined by their faith. It is bigger than that. So I would start their book as a story of love.

I think their story has universal appeal because the principles of Lori and Bob's story apply to any big challenge. This is why this story has meaning. I think I hear in Lori's story things that are bigger than she. I think in all great stories that I read there is a deeper level of connection beyond the details of the plot. Somehow, soul-to-soul, we connect. I think there are things in this story that will touch you, even if you don't have Parkinson's. You can draw inspiration from hearing this story, even though you are not living it. I told Lori and Bob, "As I hear you speaking about your story, for me there are clearly spiritual things, issues of faith."

There are many books written about spiritual journeys that in my opinion overspiritualize things. It's not necessary to talk about everything in terms of God: God is doing this, God is doing that. I think Lori and Bob are a couple who believe that spirituality ultimately leaves faith in the realm of mystery.

The great Carroll Wise said pastoral care is the art of bringing the inner meaning of the Gospel to people at their point of need. What I love in his definition is the concept of the inner meaning of the Gospel. It's not ideology. It's not a belief system. It is the inner meaning, the human encounter with the divine, the sense of paths unknown, the mystery of life, meeting particular individual people in particular places in their life's journey. So ministry then is to bring the inner meaning of the Gospel to people at their point of need. My ministry is not my telling people, "I will tell you what needs to happen here: you need to get converted; you need to find faith; you need to find Jesus." As a result, ministry becomes about helping you do what you need to do. It is bringing the meaning of the Gospel to what it is that you need. It is not to change your need or to change who you are.

If the inner meaning of the Gospel is one side of the equation, I think Bob and Lori fall on the other side of the equation—more in the direction of life is a beautiful mystery. It is bigger than any one of us. It is bigger than any combination of us. It is bigger than any time in the human experience. So what we all do is strive to connect to that mystery and to live life authentically, fully, zestfully, knowing there are no promises. Faith is not life insurance against adversity, because if it is, then when I cash in my insurance policy, I have nothing.

The three of us spoke of many things, including last summer when we feared Lori was almost at the end. And it didn't happen. After the crucifixion Easter comes, and with it the transformative process. As Lori talked, I heard messages of courage and of her relationship with Bob. She said, "*We* are facing this, *we* are going to do whatever it takes, *we* are going to do whatever *we* need to." They are fighting this fight together.

In their journey together, Bob and Lori are breathing, studying, reflecting, praying, sharing the array of interests that they have. They have the courage to refuse to submit. Courage that is not blind to the reality of Parkinson's. In my experience, I have worked with people whose coping method is sometimes to deny. That is not how Lori and Bob cope. Their courage is to face a hard reality head-on, to not diminish, to not demur, to not submit, but to draw upon inner strength of character.

I think their spiritual strength is ultimately anchored in hope—the sense of hope that no matter what the outcome, life is good. As far as spiritual strength, Lori and Bob don't expect favors from God. They do not subscribe to the kind of theology that is bartering with God. Instead, they have an acceptance of the reality of their lives. Obviously Lori wants to live. She wants to have as full a life as she can, for as long as she can. Even if this is an illness ultimately from which she does not recover and it's the illness from which she will die, still Lori wants to live as best she can as long as she can. Lori's hope is to do that. And if that doesn't happen, she is not going to be angry with God or life or the mystery because that is what the reality of life is. There are no guarantees. We all want a full, exciting, enriched life, but that doesn't happen for the vast majority of human beings on this planet.

Lori feels blessed and spiritually strong, in the sense of living with a perspective that life doesn't have any guarantees and that she is going to give it all she has and hope for the best. Within this perspective, she knows she is truly a blessed person.

Life has given her Parkinson's, yet she and Bob are pretty much the same after the disease as they were before she was diagnosed in terms of character, of the things that I would use to describe them. They were fully present before the Parkinson's and during the Parkinson's. I think that is how they navigate life.

Lori and Bob are people who have deep faith. Their faith is principally faith in each other. They know they can be trusted, and they can trust each other. They are loyal to each other. They are dedicated to each other. They are compassionate about each other. They have faith in the human family. When people talk, for example, about the downside of the economy or what is happening in the world, Bob and Lori always look for the way out. They do not look at the situation with rose-colored glasses that deny the risks and the dangers of the dark side of things, but they look for a solution. And to me, that is the deepest kind of faith. It is not ideological faith. Faith is not what you believe; faith is what you are.

Because faith is what we are, our beliefs will change over time as we evolve. Bob and Lori are people of faith because of who they are, not because of what they believe. I don't even think they believe in the same things. But it doesn't matter because real faith transcends that. My own late wife and I didn't believe the same things, but our love transcended that. It was bigger than the things we believed or didn't believe. We changed our positions as we influenced each other, but we evolved and we were dynamic. I think that Lori and Bob are two people who embody faith in each other and who always look to the good.

I think Lori and Bob's story is the story of who these two people are, their character structure, their inner world, their inner fiber. It happens to play out in Parkinson's, but it plays out as a mirror of the people they are. It was playing out in their lives long before Parkinson's, and it will play out through Parkinson's and beyond. I think that is how I would characterize their faith.

In psychology, one of the measures of the health of the ego is how resilient it is. Developing resilience is the definition of psychological health. I think the same is true in spiritual life. We always regress; sometimes we are sad or sorrowful. How quickly we come back without being defensive and needing to deny the reality that we feel—that is resilience. Let me explain what I mean by resilience by telling you something my trainer told me. The trainer said to me, "You know, Bob, being in shape doesn't mean that your body doesn't undergo stress. Being in shape means your body bounces back quickly, your heart rate returns to normal quickly. A person who is in shape returns to normal faster than the person who is out of shape." That is what I mean by resilience—bouncing back after stress. Certainly Lori and Bob have done that again and again.

Last summer Lori experienced a miracle. I think Lori and Bob accept with humility this "miracle," or this privilege that the gift of life has extended to them, as I like to put it. In this sense, her remission is a miracle, but not a miracle in the regressive sense of a simplistic world where God makes interventions and spares some people. We don't know why miracles happen. In the grand scheme it is not for us to question. To me this is where Lori and Bob live. They live in a grander place.

APPENDIX

Cheryl Becker's Log of Lori Patin's Surgeries, Accidents, and Difficult Events

Dec. 1997   Diagnosed with Parkinson's.
Oct. 2000   First Feldenkrais Method[9] lesson.

Long history of falls. Fell on her knees many times as a child. Fell down stairs. Fell out of trees while picking fruit. Has scar on left foot from injury that occurred when she was twenty-one.

Broke her tailbone four times: First time: Fell during high school play. Since her grandmother had recently broken hers and said it was excruciating to have the doctor put it back, Lori decided not to visit doctor. Second time, 1966: Tobogganing accident. Third time, 1972: Playing tennis. Fourth time, 1997: Fell off ladder and landed on paint can.

Oct. 2000   Surgery to put pins, plates, and rods in wrist broken from fall.
Nov. 2000   Pins removed.
June 2001   Fell at curb prior to Feldenkrais® lesson.
June 2001   Fell on basket that dog knocked down steps.
July 2002   Didn't see a curb in parking lot, stumbled, and fell without injury.

---

[9]   Feldenkrais Method® and Guild Certified Feldenkrais Practitioner® are registered trademarks of The Feldenkrais Guild®.

Oct. 2002   Tripped twice and fell.

Dec. 2002   Tripped over same curb as in July. Dislocated little finger of left hand.

Feb. 2003   Fell on tailbone, tripping over stack of bags at ankle height.

July 2003   Trips because right foot doesn't lift high enough and left foot drags.

June 2003   Her mother dies.

Feb. 2005   Wrenched low back, bending down and twisting to pick up paper.

July 2005   Short of breath upon exertion.

Mar. 2006   Had one episode of shortness of breath. Doctors attribute to PD. Message from brain to respiratory muscles slow.

June 2006   Fell going upstairs. Ribs feel askew.

July 2006   Fell tripping on edge of sidewalk and driveway and again going up stairs. Only puts toes on stair. Doesn't bend ankle enough. Going down stairs, often sees only a "pathway," not the edges of steps.

Oct. 2006   Occasional spells of shortness of breath while climbing stairs.

Nov. 2006   Doctor says her eyes do not team properly.

May 2007   Tripped on step, fell forward on face onto cement, hit top of head on wall. Facial cuts around mouth.

June 2007   Falls.

June 2007   Trips and falls.

July 2007   Tripped going upstairs.

Oct. 2007   Stubbed left second toe three times on stair risers. Broke toe. Doctor says toe has been broken and jammed many times and will probably need surgery.

Jan. 2008   Surgery to reassemble joint of second toe on left foot.

Mar. 2008   Surgery to remove infection in toe joint.

Sep. 2008   Hospitalized because passed out in elevator. Doctors don't know why.

Jan. 2009   Cataract surgery on right eye. Two weeks later, cataract surgery on left eye.

May 2009   Tripped over watering hose "with trippy shoes." Fell forward onto hands and knees. Broke bones in wrists.

Mar. 2010   Tripped and hit left side of forehead.

July 2010   Chemical stress test found slight abnormality in heart, "nothing serious."

Aug. 2010   Blood pressure drops precipitously. Doctors don't know why and don't want to change Parkinson's meds because lowering the dosage would cause more PD symptoms. Fell during harp lesson. Dehydration apparently caused meds to interact adversely.

Aug. 2010   Tripped on outdoor steps and hit left side of head on planter pot. Emergency medics determined she was okay.

Sep. 2010   Dropped suddenly twice. First time, on way to seats in stadium. Fell on field but didn't hit head. Knew she needed to bend down so took a controlled fall. Breathing hard. Second time, after two hours in sun without hydration. Fell inside ladies' room stall and couldn't speak until she got up from floor. Saw stars.

Sep. 2010   After sprinkling flowers with watering can, headed for sofa to lie down but collapsed on stairs before she got there.

Feb. 2011   Hospitalized for breathing issues. Doctors installed pacemaker to keep heart rate high enough to support both blood pressure and breathing issues.

June 2011   Hospitalized with complications from PD meds. Went into rare kind of coma called a spindle coma, emerging from the first to go into another the following day. Diagnostics suggest that may be caused by Lewy body disease. Stabilized and transferred to Mather Pavilion for rehab.

Dec. 2011   BIG NEWS. Lori's neurologist says Lori's Parkinson's has reversed direction. Getting better. Doctor says she still has PD but less than before. Meds reduced.

LORI'S LESSONS

OVER THE LAST FIFTEEN YEARS, Parkinson's has taught me many lessons. While I wish I hadn't had to learn them, they have brought me comfort, strength, and blessings. Although I'm shy by nature and have never been one to give unsolicited advice (except to Bob and my kids), I've conceded to pressure from family, caregivers, and friends to share what I and we have learned. I humbly offer them to you because they have taught me so much about life itself and continue to help me fight against my disease. And I hope you too will benefit from them when life throws challenges at you.

1) When you are under attack, you must attack back . . . in your personal, maybe even very quiet way. If you run away, your challenge will catch you from behind and eat you. Relentless determination is the only omnipotent force in a tough fight. You can wear down your opponent; you've just got to want to win more.

2) The bravest thing you can do is to believe that bravery exists and act accordingly.

3) The two best drugs in the world are hope and faith. Hope for the best, plan for the worst, and have faith that there are forces at work that are with you and forever on your side.

4) Hope creates hope. If you have hope, you will keep fighting, which creates positive results, which creates more hope—a positively reinforcing cycle. The opposite is also true: if you lose hope, you stop trying, which creates losing results—a negatively reinforcing cycle.

5) Attitude is everything. Don't just spend the rest of your life feeling sorry for yourself, sitting in a corner waiting for the worst to happen. Instead, keep in mind that this is the one life you have and decide to make the best of it. Within the parameters of your particular challenge, the only thing you can control is yourself. Life has no real guarantees. Live with the perspective that says, "I'll give it all I've got and hope for the best."

6) Make constant "deposits" into your energy bank accounts with hugs, sunrises, and laughs. They will allow for big withdrawals when you get hit with the unexpected.

7) Be grateful for every gift. I say a prayer each time I look at the flowers that grow from the seeds I planted.

8) Own and accept your situation. Don't deny full ownership or lie to others about it. Being honest with yourself about your challenge allows you to confront it rather than to hide, which just wastes time, energy, and resources. Being honest with your friends draws not scorn or isolation but sympathy, prayers, resources, and ideas to support your fight. You will be amazed at the forces that come your way if you just share your story.

9) Seek out communities that will nurture you. Communities are an extension and reflection of the family and they enhance life. Belong to a community, and it will celebrate with your joy and commiserate with your pain. You need the members of the community for support, and they need you as a good example. Expect to be responsible to and for the community, just as it is responsible to and for you. Isolation is a killer, and inclusion is a savior.

10) Set goals—realistic, achievable, but challenging goals. Goals will move you forward because they create tension between where you are and where you want to go. But you may have to redefine success. Before you got blindsided by your challenge, you measured success in certain ways. Now your situation may make you measure success

differently. Before I had PD, I was an aerobics instructor. Now I am proud to be able to go ballroom dancing.

11) Decide what is really important in your life—whether it's being with family and friends, or gardening, or writing your memoirs—and make sure you spend time doing it.

12) Give some things up. You will be surprised what you will gain. I gave up some of my independence, and it has brought me so much closer to my family and friends.

13) Miracles are surely sometimes given from on high, but don't count on that kind of miracle. The most likely miracles are the ones you will create yourself with hard work and a good attitude.

Lessons for Caregiving:

1) If you can afford to pay for help, get it. Don't be afraid to experiment, but don't do anything really dumb or risky. If you can't afford to pay, ask friends and family. People are willing, even anxious to help. Conquer your embarrassment because the little mistake is to ask and be turned down, but the big mistake is to never ask and miss getting help.

2) Accepting help is not a sign of weakness but of strength. It takes strength to accept your limitations and to allow someone to assist you. To ask for and receive help requires the powerful combination of humility and courage.

3) Communicate. Don't expect anyone to guess what you want and need, or don't want and dislike. Mean what you say and say what you mean.

4) It is in everyone's selfish best interest to demand that your caregivers take care of themselves. It is a good idea for you also to take care of them to the best of your abilities. They can and will wear out if both they and you are not careful.

5) Your caregivers will come to realize that when the person they love and care for has a difficult challenge, so do they.

Of course the degree of ownership involved is different. Even though the challenge is primarily yours, it will confront your caregivers and affect them too. They can even make it work for both of you if they think about it the right way.

6) Make sure your caregiver has something else in his or her life to give him or her fulfillment. A steady diet of you/you/you will get a bit stale. He or she will return refreshed after doing whatever it is that interests him or her.

7) The biggest challenge for your caregiver is to hate the disease, really loathe it, but not resent the person who has it. He or she may know intellectually that it is not your fault, but every caregiver has moments of thinking, *Why me? What did I do to deserve this?* They have to set that aside and move on, for themselves as much as for you. Still, to underestimate the challenge of dealing with their emotions would be not only naïve but potentially destructive.

8) You must love the people who love you. Their love and care demands reciprocity. You can't just expect or demand or even accept their love and care without convincing them that you love them back. If nothing else, *just tell them*!

Lori Cedik and Bob Patin did not get off to an auspicious start. Although it almost didn't happen, their first date was the best date of their lives. Time was short but they made the most of it. Four months after they started dating, she left for California to teach and he for Cleveland to work for Connecticut General. True love overcame time and distance, with the aid of many so-called "horny" telephone calls.

On August 14, 1965, Lori and Bob took their vows, very sure of each other no matter what the future might hold. As much as they loved each other on that day in August, it was romantic kid-stuff compared to the feelings they have for each other now.

Aly, left, was born in 1971, and Jen came fifteen months later. In this picture the Patins' smiling daughters are five and three and a half. Lori devoted herself to raising the girls. Alone much of the time with Bob traveling for work, she had to "develop skills and attitudes that have served me and us well, especially now as I fight my disease."

A mother, an aerobics instructor, and a "beach property" landlord,
Lori enjoyed life during the '80s and '90s. Unfortunately
Parkinson's was lurking. In 1987, with a disconcerting
trembling in her left hand, her enemy reared its ugly head.

In 1997, Lori received the diagnosis of Parkinson's disease. Her cruel
opponent was here to stay. After a few months of tears, she realized
that Parkinson's wasn't going to kill her, and she was determined to
make the best of her life. Lori dug in to fight, with Bob alongside her
in every battle. One way they combat her disease is to dance together,
both to have fun and to work on Lori's balance on the ballroom floor.

A proud clansman, Bob wore his kilt to Aly's wedding in 2001. Lori had so many tremors from Parkinson's that she had a hard time keeping her balance walking down the aisle even with Bob to help her. Aly said, "I knew at that point Parkinson's had taken its toll." Ten years later at a party for Aly's husband's family, Matt's relatives didn't recognize Lori at first because she was so much better. They applauded while she danced.

Never Surrender

The summer of 2011, Lori lay in a coma. Bob began looking into nursing homes, but Lori made up her mind to get better. Her attitude is: "I'll give it all I've got and hope for the best." Now she has fewer symptoms than she had in 2001. Her doctor, Michael Rezak, a nationally known Parkinson's specialist, says he has never seen such an improvement in a Parkinson's patient. Above her desk, she hangs a cartoon similar to this one by her grandson Payton Witherell.

Lori takes tai chi lessons to improve her balance. She attacks her
implacable foe with a full arsenal, relying upon both Western
and Eastern medicine, exercising several hours a day, and doing
deep-tissue massage, acupuncture, and Feldenkrais® weekly.

Lori lives life to the fullest, Parkinson's be damned. Here she's fly-fishing for trout. Lori is grateful for every gift and "makes constant 'deposits' into her energy bank accounts with hugs, sunrises, and laughs."

The Patins have developed a morning ritual that brings them great joy. Bob makes Lori's breakfast and brings it to her on a tray. Then he helps her shower and blow-dries her hair. The girls joke Lori gets her hair done at Chez Robert (pronounced shay ro-BEAR). Bob finds special meaning in this cartoon by his grandson Payton Witherell.

Today both Aly and Jen live within a half hour of their parents. Lori feels blessed that her daughters and their children are such a big part of her life. They take turns staying with her when Bob travels for business. They share the sorrows, joys, and burdens of Parkinson's with Lori and Bob.

Lori says, "I would not be alive without Bob." Bob
says, "I wouldn't want to live without Lori."